The Emotion Devotional

40 Day Journey

Toward Emotional Wholeness

QuaVaundra Perry, PhD, ABPP

FIRST EDITION

www.drqperry.com

Unless otherwise noted, all Scripture quotations are taken from the Holman Christian Standard Bible®, Used by Permission HCSB ©1999,2000,2002,2003,2009 Holman Bible Publishers. Holman Christian Standard Bible®, Holman CSB®, and HCSB® are federally registered trademarks of Holman Bible Publishers.

Scripture quotations taken from the Amplified Bible (AMP), Copyright © 2015 by The Lockman Foundation. Used by permission. www.Lockman.org.

Scripture quotations marked (GNT) are from the Good News Translation in Today's English Version- Second Edition Copyright © 1992 by American Bible Society. Used by Permission.

Scriptures quotations marked (NASB) are taken from the New American Standard Bible® (NASB), Copyright © 1960, 1962, 1963, 1968, 1971, 1972, 1973, 1975, 1977, 1995 by The Lockman Foundation. Used by permission. www.Lockman.org.

Scripture quotations marked (NLT) are taken from the Holy Bible, New Living Translation, copyright ©1996, 2004, 2015 by Tyndale House Foundation. Used by permission of Tyndale House Publishers, a Division of Tyndale House Ministries, Carol Stream, Illinois 60188. All rights reserved.

Scriptures quotations marked (KJV) are taken from the King James Version. Public domain.

Scripture quotations marked (TPT) are taken from The Passion Translation®. Copyright © 2017, 2018 by Passion & Fire Ministries, Inc. Used by permission. All rights reserved. ThePassionTranslation.com.

IMPORTANT NOTICE TO READER:
This book contains opinions and ideas of its author and has been written and published for informational and educational purposes only. It is sold with the understanding that the author is not engaged in rendering medical, mental health, or any other kind of personal professional services in the book. The advice and strategies contained herein may not be suitable for every situation. If professional assistance is required, the services of a competent professional personal should be sought. The author specifically disclaims all responsibility for any liability, loss, or risk – personal or otherwise – that is incurred as a consequence, directly or indirectly, by the use and application of any of the contents of this book. Readers should be aware that any websites or other materials are listed as a reference only and not an endorsement by the author. Readers should also be aware that websites may have changed or disappeared between the time this work was written and when it is read.

Case examples are composites of cases from Dr. Perry's clinical practice. Names and circumstances have been changed to protect privacy.

ISBN: 978-1-7344543-0-7

DEDICATION

To my mother and for my son.

TABLE OF CONTENTS

The
Emotion
Devotional

40 Day Journey

Toward Emotional Wholeness

INTRODUCTION:

Hi there! I am so glad you're here.

The *Emotion Devotional* was dropped in my spirit during a very critical time in my life as I was in several major transitions. To begin, I had just buried my mother after caring for her for 8 years. I was also in deep prayer about leaving my job to pursue full-time entrepreneurship and examining many of my close personal relationships. Prior to that, I'd dealt with a lot of other incidents in both my personal and professional worlds. All things considered, I'd say these past 5 years have been…well, emotional. Full of dream-come-true mountains and expected valleys, sprinkled with surprising elevations and unexpected troughs. I can surely say my faith has been tested, and I have grown spiritually. One thing that has been interesting to me, though, is the new range of emotions I experienced over those years. Wait! That doesn't make sense. How was I growing spiritually but also feeling unlike myself at times? In addition to spiritual maturity, I realized God was helping me to emotionally develop too. Yes, spiritual and emotional maturity are connected. God was revealing things in my heart that I didn't know were there and/or He was equipping me to relate to the people I serve.

Dear friend, I believe you are one of the people God was preparing me to help. See, I think I know your story. I may not know the specifics, but I know you're a smart, ambitious, and goal-driven Christian. Nonetheless, there's this other part of you that's hard to manage. Your emotions. You silently (or loudly for some) struggle to carry the emotional baggage from situations in your life. On the one hand, you love God and want to grow closer to Him, but something stands in the way. You want to grow deeper in your relationship with others, but you keep running into stumbling blocks. On the other hand, life may have dealt you some serious blows, and you're not sure you want to be close to people anymore. Yet, you know deep inside that's not God's plan for you.

In *The Emotion Devotional*, I wanted to mix my training, knowledge, and experiences with my revelations from God to give you (and me) a resource to address those parts of your life that are normally compartmentalized. There's no shortage of resources about mental wellness and spiritual growth. The challenge is finding out how to combine the two in a way that is practical and relevant.

Within these pages, you will find an uncomfortable yet life-changing treat. I want to take you on a journey towards emotional wholeness. I'll admit some of my patients have been frustrated with me at the beginning of our work together because they came in looking for shortcuts, quick skills, tips, and steps to solve their problems. I believe real change happens at the heart level, and that takes time. To your surprise, there are no devotions about pleasant emotions in this book. I specifically aimed to focus on the unpleasant emotions and thoughts that keep us stuck in cycles.

What are emotions anyway? In psychology, we like to drill down the definition of words so we can make sure we're all on the same page for the discussion. The nuances we assign to words and experiences have led to different theories about emotions, feelings, and thoughts. As such, I initially considered introducing this book with a quick discussion on the difference between thoughts, feelings, emotions, and attitudes. I was also going to include a brief summary of some studies on these concepts. However, the further I went down the rabbit hole, I realized that approach is beyond the heartbeat of this book. What difference would it make to have a scholarly definition of every emotion in the book and still struggle to manage your emotions and their impact on your life? I wanted the focus of this book to be about the unpleasant feelings and associated thoughts that challenge you daily. The goal is to make these concepts understandable and relevant to your everyday walk with God.

Speaking of goals, I see that word everywhere I look these days. We are asked on a daily basis about our entrepreneurial goals, relationship goals, health goals, and financial goals. How can you have relationship goals without knowing how to communicate your feelings? How can you sustain financial and health accomplishments when you don't understand the emotions that are driving you to spend and eat the way you do? Don't get me wrong. Having goals is valuable and necessary, but I think life is about more than just meeting goals. The journey towards obtaining your hopes and dreams is what can make or break you. Do you know why? Because life happens along the way and you have an emotional response to what happens to you.

Ready to get started?

FIRST THINGS, FIRST

In my work, one of the first lessons I teach is how to accurately label and express emotions. This is an important step where I spend a lot of time because I have noticed our emotion vocabulary tends to be very limited or imprecise. Here's what I mean. When asked how you feel, do you say, "*Good, fine, okay, blessed, or alright?*" You might also say something along the lines of "*I feel like she was wrong for what she said*" or "*I felt that he was inconsiderate.*" If your answer includes "like or that," it's a thought, not a feeling. Learning to describe and voice your emotions can feel uncomfortable at first, especially if you're accustomed to denying them or glossing over them by saying you feel "some kind of way." It's a powerful tool that takes your communication to the next level.

The 40 words in *The Emotion Devotional* are the main emotion vocabulary words I start with in my work, and I want to share them with you. I want us to move beyond basic emotions like mad, sad, and happy (though some of them are in the book). My hope is that you'll recognize there is actually a range of emotions that better paints the picture of your internal reactions. Of course, there are more than 40 feeling words, but the ones in this book are a great way to get started.

Once you learn how to properly identify your emotions, you will be well on your way to effectively articulating them to God and to others. My prayer is that as your emotional vocabulary increases, your emotional awareness will increase. Then you'll be able to better manage your mood and not allow it to control your behavior. You won't have to resort to unhealthy ways of coping like shutting down, withdrawing from God and others or excessive shopping, exercising, drinking, eating, makeup, sex, or working.

My other prayer is that as you mature emotionally, you'll grow spiritually. If we can better manage our emotions, it won't be so easy for Satan to sift us like wheat (Luke 22:31-32). During the sifting is when we lose heart due to our natural emotional reaction to painful circumstances. We believe and act upon our feelings because they are so strong and compelling. The good news is that Jesus has already prayed that our faith does not fail us (v.32a). We have to do our part by returning to Him and eventually using our spiritual and emotional maturity to strengthen others.

A 40-DAY JOURNEY

Devotionals come in a variety of lengths ranging from 21 to 365 days. At first, I wasn't sure which length would be suitable for the content and purpose of *The Emotion Devotional*. After praying and studying, I sensed God leading me towards a 40-day experience. Forty days signifies trial before triumph. Recall Jesus was led by the Spirit to the wilderness, and He did not eat physical food the entire time He was there (Matt. 4:1-11). Can you imagine his physical and emotional state? The enemy made Him all kinds of offers in this state of vulnerability. What he didn't realize was that Jesus' physical weakness was no indication of His spiritual and emotional determination. After Jesus was tempted privately, He began His public ministry. God is not haphazard in the details of our lives. As such, I believe we can see more outward success if we begin to master our private lives (i.e., emotions).

You will notice the subtitle says *toward* emotional wholeness and not *to* emotional wholeness. That's because my expectation is not that you'll be magically cured of all unpleasant emotions in 40 days. Plus, the aim of this book is not to prevent you from ever feeling unpleasant emotions again, but that you'll learn to recognize them and take the associated thoughts captive. While you may be quickly delivered from the stronghold of some thoughts and feelings, there may be others that will be laborious and last well beyond 40 days. You may also recognize the need for some outside help from a spiritual leader or mental health professional.

HOW TO USE THE EMOTION DEVOTIONAL

The book is structured such that there is 1 emotion covered per day. It is introduced by a definition or synonyms, followed by a key Scripture(s). The daily reading associated with the emotion includes ideas, steps, or questions to provoke thought and healing on your journey towards emotional wholeness. Each passage ends with a prayer designed to help deepen your conversations with God.

While *The Emotion Devotional* is structured for 40 days, there's no 1 right way to use the book. Some people may prefer to read it straight through by tackling one emotion a day. Others may want to start at the beginning and spend time processing and praying through what they've read over the course of days or weeks. Some people may desire to only pick out the emotions that are most relevant to their current situation. Others might prefer to explore the emotions that are not the most prevalent. Whichever method you choose, I recommend having a couple of items with you including a paper and pen for notes and your Bible for reference. You might also want a dictionary or thesaurus. As you read, I invite you to unplug from the daily grind and tune into your soul and spirit. Seriously contemplate the questions that come up for you and the impressions God puts in your heart.

I should alert you *The Emotion Devotional* might cause you to explore some feelings you've suppressed or identify the ones you've never acknowledged. Let me encourage you not to criticize or judge yourself. I often hear my patients preface their feelings with, "*I know*

I'm wrong for feeling this way" or *"I shouldn't feel like this."* Try to think of your emotions (and your response to them) as effective/ineffective, workable/not workable, or helpful/unhelpful rather than right or wrong. Sometimes our experience turns from pain to suffering because we judge our feelings.

God's word tells us that He has given us a sound mind (2 Tim. 1:7). The Amplified version interprets this to mean a "personal discipline that results in a calm well-balanced mind and self-control." My friend, I desire for you to think...grow...and live a full and meaningful life!

Day 1

ANGRY

Feeling anger, a strong feeling of dissatisfaction in response to a painful situation.

A fool gives full vent to his anger, but a wise man holds it in check.
PROVERBS 29:11

There's a profound quote from a poem by the late Eleanor Roosevelt that says, *"Anger is one letter short of danger."* This short statement reminds us of the power of anger. What or who comes to mind when you hear the word anger? Chances are, you think of terrorists or mass shooters, people with road rage, the mother who harshly disciplines her children, or the guy who can't tolerate losing a game and punches his opponent. While these are certainly models of anger, it is important to understand anger does not always manifest in volatile ways. Consider this scenario in Tim and Christina's relationship:

> *As Christina cooks dinner, she tells Tim she does not feel loved and she is tired of him spending so much time with his friends. Tim feels frustrated because he can never satisfy Christina, so he does not respond at all. When this happens, Christina feels even more hurt and shows it by yelling and breaking dishes. Tim leaves the house and posts a snarky message on social media.*

Which partner do you think has an anger problem? Does your anger look more like Christina's (*aggressive*) or Tim's (*passive-aggressive*)? If you don't see yourself in either style, you probably fall into a 3rd category like many Christians: *passive*. Let me explain.

When I was younger, I had the reputation of letting everything that hit my heart, hit my tongue (I may or may not have been called "a little firecracker"). As I've matured, I have worked hard to offer grace with my words and to consider timing in what I say. I can tell the difference it makes to honor God and others by speaking the truth with love (Eph. 4:26-32). In this way, respect for myself and others is preserved and it increases the likelihood of being heard. The other person may not agree with what I'm saying, but that's okay.

Regrettably, there have been times when I have taken that approach too far by ignoring, avoiding, and denying my feelings, including anger. I believe we regularly presume God does not ever want us to voice anger and assume being a "good Christian" means we should tolerate mistreatment from others. How freeing it was when my mother reminded me that is not God's plan for me! Now, I'm passing on that wisdom to you. That is not God's plan for you either.

Feeling angry is not a sin. In fact, anger is usually the fruit of something with deeper roots like hurt, offense, betrayal, or rejection. For many people, it is an easier emotion to access and express than more vulnerable emotions. If the Word says to be angry and sin not (Eph. 4:26), it must mean the sin comes in how we express it. Our key verse indicates it is foolish to fully vent your anger in an uncontrolled way.

Test out these helpful anger management strategies:

1. Identify your anger style and submit it to the Lord.

2. Learn to spot the secondary emotions behind anger.

3. Practice communicating vulnerable emotions, so they do not take root and manifest unhealthy fruit.

> *God, thank You for being an example of love in the midst of my shortcomings. I aim to have temperance and wisdom in my expression of anger. Thank You for making space for healing in my relationships with others.*

Day 2

ANXIOUS

A fearful emotional state about an actual or potential future situation.

Can any of you add a cubit to his height by worrying?
LUKE 12:25

A good friend of mine once described my mind as a clock, and it's such an accurate metaphor to the continuous nature of my mind. It never stops. I could try to dress it up by saying I'm a planner, I like to stay organized, and I like to be prepared. Yes, those characteristics are true and generally positive, but the reality is that I feel anxious sometimes and I hate it. I don't like it when my planning and preparation leads me to step into God's territory of wanting to know the future right now.

What's frustrating is when people tell you, "just don't worry about it," because it's not that easy. I'm sure you feel the same way. You wish anxiety didn't keep you from walking in the peace God gave us. What do you worry about? Here's what's repeatedly in my worry catalog: **Career, Child, Faith, Family, Finances, Friends, Health, & Relationships**. The order in which they appear depends on the day, right? As someone who studies and treats anxiety, I had never had an epiphany about anxiety like I had a few months ago.

I was driving alone down the highway when a question popped in my mind. *Does worrying really work?* Think about it. When I worry, my mind frets a variety of potential situations, and then I tell myself I need to be prepared. I "pray" and then try to do all I can to fix or avoid whatever I'm worried about. I mean faith without works is dead, right? Any time I have put a lot of work into something, it is productive. Yet, I don't get those same results when I worry. Instead, I'm unproductive because I'm consumed with "what ifs" and I experience other problems like poor sleep, difficulty concentrating, and restlessness. Some anxiety is normal and can even be useful but when it disturbs your functioning is when it becomes problematic. I'm curious to know if worrying really works for you? I mean does it *really* work. Our key verse tells us that worrying does not accomplish anything at all.

So how can you start the process of releasing your anxiety?

1) **Recognize ways anxiety shows up in your life.** Your self-proclaimed label of being an organizer, Type A personality, or high-strung could actually be anxiety that's not working for you.

2) **Understand there's a difference between probability and possibility.** Just because something could happen doesn't mean it will happen. Anything is possible, but not everything is probable. Here's the beauty in whatever you're worried about. God is able. He is the God of the impossible.

3) **Give God your list of 'what ifs'.** *What if I can't have a baby? What if my children get off course? What if my wife decides not to reconcile the relationship? What if my business fails? What if I never get married. What if the test comes back positive? What if I don't get the job?* For the person who's like me who just has to know all the details, I want to encourage you to trust God

with the details. I had to get myself off the throne and realize I'm not God, so I don't need to know all the details.

4) **Don't make matters worse.** Our pain can turn to suffering when we beat ourselves up with negative self-talk (e.g., *I must not be a true Christian because I'm anxious.*). It's a signal that you can tell God you're still worried and ask for His peace and reassurance.

Trying these steps won't be a one-and-done method but will take practice. I love how God doesn't judge us for having certain unhelpful emotions, and neither should we judge ourselves. When the Scripture says, be anxious for nothing, it means don't carry the weight of worrying about matters all by yourself (Phil. 4:6 NASB). He wants you to tell Him your worries, your true requests about the matter, and then thank Him for hearing your prayer. When your mind begins to wonder, wander, ruminate, obsess, and reason, it means you have started to lean to your own (limited) understanding. Let God do what He does best…being a God who never changes and works all things out for our good (Rom. 8:28).

> *God, please forgive me for worrying about what I should readily and repeatedly hand over to You. Increase my awareness of my anxious thoughts and my attempts to fix them. Help my unbelief. I want to walk and rest in Your peace. Thank You for being trustworthy.*

Day 3

BETRAYED

To be disloyal to; To disappoint the expectations of.

If you do what is good to those who are good to you,
what credit is that to you? Even sinners do that.
LUKE 6:33

May I be transparent? Once in a while, it seems as though God wants too much from me. Imagine this situation I was in. There was a young lady who surprisingly befriended me. I say surprisingly because it was an unexpected friendship since I was unlike her regular group of friends. She was kind and thoughtful, and as our relationship developed, she began sharing some personal struggles. I could sense her sadness, so I began to pray for her. She was such a sweetheart, and I wanted God to give her the desires of her heart. Well, I was completely caught off guard when I found out not only had she been talking badly about me but even making fun of me. I felt confused and betrayed! My first thought was, *"I can easily fix this by cutting her off."* Then God intervened and gave me no peace about that approach. Not only was I forbidden from removing her from my life but God didn't even let me give her the stink eye. Sigh!! Really, God??

It took some time to surrender my emotions since everything in me felt betrayed and rebellious. Something in me told me that she would need to confide in me again in the future, so I could not let her or my fleshly nature ruin my spiritual witness. This was definitely not an easy task! In fact, it was just the opposite. There were times when the memory of what she did felt fresh, and I wanted to be mad at her. When I wanted to seek revenge, I had to continuously lay those feelings of betrayal before the Lord. God is so faithful, and I rejoiced when the day actually came for her to ask me to pray for her. I was glad that I could genuinely and earnestly intercede for her.

I did not share that story to suggest that God wants you to remain connected to everyone who has betrayed you. What I am saying is that God will use betrayal to stretch you in ways that are uncomfortable but for your ultimate good. I'm not sure of the source of your betrayal, but I encourage you to seek God for direction on how to respond as the answers are not always black and white. Naturally, when people are nice to you, you're nice to them, and when they're not, you're not. It's easy to love those who are behaving in ways that are loveable. It seems like a simple formula, right? When we operate the way our fleshly instincts encourage us to do, we miss opportunities to grow in our faith. God calls us to a higher standard according to the verses that follow our key verse (Luke 6:35). Being good to those who are not good to you demonstrates a level of emotional and spiritual maturity. God knows we cannot do this in our own strength, so He works in us to will and to do what pleases Him (Phil. 2:13 NLT).

It is important to be aware that betrayal does not only come from family, friends, significant others, children, parents, teammates, or coworkers who have cheated, lied, or stolen from us. Feeling betrayed can come from the unlikeliest of places like yourself and God. It's a real challenge to work through the pain of blaming yourself for the decisions you've made. It's frustrating when your body does not get pregnant or recover from illness or injuries in the timeframe you expected. You may even call God's loyalty into question when your prayers go unanswered. When I feel betrayed, I have reaped the benefits of drawing near to God and making room for the Holy Spirit to console me.

While reconciliation is not always in God's plan following betrayal, His desire is for your heart not to be permanently pierced with pain. Tune into God's faithfulness and His promptings for direction.

God, I am feeling betrayed because (fill in the blank). My heart is so heavy with pain, disbelief, and distrust. Grant me the ability to see and follow Jesus as an example of how to handle betrayal. I yearn for Your strength to walk in love and peace, especially with those I find hard to love.

Day 4

BORED

To feel disinterested in your current activity or state.

Pay careful attention, then, to how you walk – not as unwise people but as wise-making the most of the time, because the days are evil.
EPHESIANS 5:15-16

Je m'ennuie. That's French for "I'm bored." Yes, everyone gets bored at times, but it's situational most of the time. For instance, you may feel bored during a flight or while listening to a dull speech, but as soon as the moment is over, the boredom subsides. This boredom I'm referring to lingers. It shows up on your job, in your relationships, in your spiritual life, in your hobbies. You can't escape it. Nothing you do seems to pique your interest for very long, but you can't quite figure out why. I've found that when one or two areas of my life are thriving, other areas are lacking or seem dull. Take a look at the categories below and see if you can discover the cause and cure for your boredom.

> *Overstimulation:* Western society promotes overstimulation by giving us endless possibilities of technology and "instant" products at our fingertips (e.g., instant meals, instant coffee, instant messages). Advertisers use core words in their marketing strategy like "speed, faster, quicker," which sells the illusion of saving time and instant gratification. After

purchasing these products, I wonder what people do with all the time they save? My guess is that it affords them even more time to be overloaded by input from news, social media, music, videos, radio and television ads, video games, phone calls, texts, and emails. Though unintentional, our brains can become wired to expect entertainment and stimulation at all times, thus leading to feeling bored when every moment is not occupied. I believe this is why many folks find it hard to be still in the presence of God.

Overstimulation can also be found in pornography consumption. When people are accustomed to getting sexual fulfillment from explicit images and videos, it leads the brain to expect instant gratification and reduce relationships to entertainment purposes only. Accordingly, many people find themselves feeling bored in their sexual relationship with their spouse and often destroy families as they are led to seek fulfillment in ungodly ways.

Idleness: People run around with so much on their to-do list but still complain of being unproductive. I suspect a large explanation is idleness. Being busy doesn't mean you're not idle. It means you might be spending your time engaged in fruitless activities like watching other people's lives and pursuing endless fun. When you buy into the message that other people's lives are better than yours or that your life should be full of constant amusement, you can start to feel bored and disinterested in your own life.

Depression: Some symptoms of depression can also mimic boredom. In particular, anhedonia is a symptom of depression, and it is an inability to find pleasure in activities one would typically find enjoyable. The key to determining whether your boredom indicates depression is to explore whether you have other symptoms such as extended periods of low mood, feelings of worthlessness and guilt, decreased motivation, and changes in sleep and appetite.

Here are some ways to remedy your boredom:

- **Learn to be still in the presence of God.** There is no one perfect formula, but it can be done by turning off digital devices, sitting alone and reading the Bible or other spiritual material, or taking a quiet walk. Start slow and be patient with yourself if your mind wanders or if you become antsy. God wants to renew, refresh, and reactivate your life.

- **Identify and walk in your purpose.** Have you discovered your purpose? If so, are you pursuing it? Do you have judgements about your purpose? Not living a purpose-driven life can lead you to get caught in an unproductive cycle. You start searching for meaning and clues by watching the lives of others and end up pursuing personal or people-pleasing goals rather than God-given goals. This busyness is really masked idleness as it often leads to unproductiveness or being successful at things and relationships that are not spiritually and emotionally fruitful.

  o If you don't know your purpose, that's okay. Look to the Creator first as He is the only One who can reveal His design for your life. Jeremiah 29:11 says, "*I*" know the plans I have for you...It does not say "*Other people know the plans I have for you*" or "*Look to other people for the plans I have for you.*" Now, this doesn't mean God won't speak through a loving parent, friend, or person of influence in your life. It means we should not rely on those resources as our sole guide for discovering our purpose.

- **Complete a time audit.** This constructive and insightful exercise will help you get a more accurate account of what consumes your time. God wants us to make the most use of our time for He knows that too much idle time or ineffective use of our time leaves room for engaging in other fruitless activities like those on the list in the previous few verses (i.e., *sexual immorality, impurities, greed, idolatry*) (Eph. 5:16).

- **Ask for help.** A mental health professional can help you address depression. A school counselor or career advisor can help you explore academic and vocational changes you need to make. A friend can help to keep you accountable for how to spend your time. A minister or spiritual leader can help you find ways to develop your relationship with God.

God, thank You for increasing my insight into the root of my boredom. If I am seeking stimulation in habits outside Your will, I ask for forgiveness. Stir my spirit to find fulfillment in ways that can truly satisfy me. I ask that You refresh my spirit and emotions so I can accomplish and pursue all You have for me. I praise You for renewing my mind and awakening the gifts in me.

Day 5

BURDENED

Heavy weighted, loaded down, oppressed.

Come to Me, all of you who are weary and burdened,
and I will give you rest.
MATTHEW 11:28

If you're reading this page, I imagine you probably have a lot on your plate. Your responsibilities include family, friends, work, health, finances, ministry, community service, etc. The list goes on and on. I get it. You're the strong and dependable one people call on for advice and help, right? I understand how you feel and what you're thinking. You feel burdened, but there's no way you can lighten the load. What if I told you that somehow, in your mission of helping and serving, you may have picked up some things along the way that are not meant for you to carry? Sit with that for a moment...

After several years of practice, I noticed a common thread in the thought pattern in many of my patients: an ungodly and unhealthy sense of responsibility. I don't say that to minimize your burdens in any way. I recognize the great obligations that come from family expectations. I understand as a child, you may have had no choice but to care for everyone due to your birth order or family circumstances. I also realize you may be a natural-born leader and caretaker. I understand how your career or leadership training benefit those you lead. Even in these truths, I think it's easy for us to unintentionally draw faulty conclusions like *"I am responsible for everything that happens to me and the people I love,"* or *"God wants me to take care of everyone and everything."* This reasoning is unhealthy and it has caused you to be loaded down by weight that is only meant for God to carry.

My friend, it's not what you carry but how you carry it. For instance, I am often asked how I can listen to people's problems all the time. The implicit assumption is that I must feel burdened since that is how they would feel in my role. I explain that my position is more than a role. It's my gift, and because God has graced and equipped me for it, it does not feel heavy. Whenever it starts to weigh on me, that is my clue that it is time to take a step back to get a different view and engage in extra self-care. I have to remind myself of 2 truths: 1) I am not God. 2) It is impossible for me to be responsible for everything and everyone, including those I love. If I have to do everything for everyone, is there any room for God? If I have to make all the sacrifices for others, doesn't that defeat the power and purpose of Jesus' death on the cross?

Give God your burdens today. When He says come unto me all, who are burdened, it means **all.** It does not mean you get to decide if its weight is something you should just handle yourself or try to fix it a little more before you turn it over it to Him. Not only does God want it all, but He can handle it all!

God, thank You for being willing and able to bear
my burdens. Guide me towards a healthy view of my
responsibilities and give me the wisdom to know when I
am carrying what should be casted on You.

Day 6

CONFUSED

Puzzlement and without clarity.

For God is not the author of confusion, but of peace.
I CORINTHIANS 14:33 (KJV)

When I look back over my life, the times when I was the most unhappy and unproductive were during seasons of confusion. I had so many unanswered questions. Why did this happen to me? Why did this person walk out of my life? Why wasn't I chosen? Why did I have this experience? We often assume that getting answers or knowing why will help us get closure and feel better. In psychology, we call this *affective forecasting*, which is foretelling how we think we will feel in the future. Research indicates we are not very good at it. We think we will be satisfied or at peace once we know the reasoning behind certain incidents. We assume we cannot move on unless and until we have more clarity about the reason for our circumstances. In my experience, it only leads to more questions and more confusion.

I have had the privilege of freeing so many Christians from the old school belief that you cannot question God. I say this respectfully, but I do not think that is true. God can handle our questions. I believe it's the posture of your heart that matters most when you're approaching Him with your questions. There is a very different tone to curiosity and declaration than interrogation and accusation. A posture of interrogation and accusation sounds like this: *"God, why did my relationship end?! You let this happen! Why didn't You tell me this was going to happen? Why are You allowing me to suffer?"* Whereas a heart of curiosity and declaration sounds like this: *"God, why did my relationship end? I feel confused about why this happened. I don't know what will happen next."*

Do you see the difference? The posture of interrogation implies God is not just and it demands answers like Job did when he became exasperated from trying to understand the cause of his suffering (see Job Chapter 31, especially verse 35). I envision God responding to this tone of prayer with thought-provoking questions like He did with Job (Job Chapters 38-39). God's responses to Job point to the idea that He doesn't owe us an explanation for our suffering, and even if He chose to answer us, our limited wisdom prevents complete understanding. In contrast, the tone of curiosity and declaration wants answers, but the questions are asked humbly. Read Judges 6:13-16 and see how Gideon expressed his confusion about their plight and his perceived weakness in facing the next task. God reminded Gideon that He is with him and will provide him the strength to win the battle.

The point I'm making here is this: it's not bad, wrong, or sinful to have questions. Our struggle comes in our expression of confusion and what it leads us to do. When we don't know all the answers, we often draw the wrong conclusions. Our brain is not inclined to like gray areas, so we lean to our own understanding.

As you search for clarity in your current situation, consider starting with the steps below:

1. Humbly express your true sentiments to God. Take it a step further by reminding yourself of God's sovereignty and faithfulness. He is not the author of confusion.

2. Understand that you can move forward without having all your questions answered.

3. Change your question from why to *what* and *how*. When I've felt stuck ruminating about the reasons why something did or didn't happen, it was incredibly helpful to ask God what He wanted me to learn about Him or myself in the situation.

God, I feel confused about (<u>fill in the blank)</u> and wished
I understood why I was going through this situation.
Thank You that You are not the author of confusion.
Hold my hand as I walk and live in Your peace. Shine
light on the wisdom I am to gain from this experience.

Day 7

CRITICAL

To feel or express judgements/harsh comments onto others.

*A gentle answer turns away anger, but a harsh
word stirs up wrath.*
PROVERBS 15:1

Several years ago, I encountered a person who was very critical. Critique here, assessment there, correction here, criticism there. I thought I could keep a positive attitude and use conflict management skills to try to find common ground. However, I just could not win! I decided at that moment that I would not be critical of others because I did not want anyone to feel the way I felt. I wish I could say I completely succeeded in that endeavor, but I have not.

I imagine you're reading this section because you have been struggling with being and feeling critical, too. Some people might not see themselves on these pages since they do not view themselves as mean or verbally abusive. Allow me to clarify that criticism can be expressed directly to the person, in conversations with others, or in inner thoughts. Regardless of how the criticism manifests, it is a matter of the heart. In my own emotional heart surgery and working with others to eradicate criticism, I discovered a number of reasons we are critical:-

- **Environment:** *You grew up in a critical atmosphere, so it became the norm to express yourself in that manner.*

- **Insecure:** *You are unhappy within yourself, so you find fault in others.*

- **Avenger:** *You think retaliation is golden. They criticize you, so it's okay to criticize them.*

- **Pride:** *You conclude your way is best.*

The list doesn't end there. I was astounded when God showed me criticism can also be a misuse of your gift of discernment. For instance, you sense someone is struggling with a particular issue, and rather than pray for the person, you display contempt and criticize them harshly. You may have some ideas about how they should handle a situation but ultimately, God is the only One who is omniscient. Offer your words of wisdom with humility, grace and truth. Having a critical spirit affects us by robbing us of peace, separating us from others (Prov. 16:28 NASB), and stirring up anger (Prov. 15:1).

If you are struggling with criticism, try using the following strategies:

1. **Identify themes in your criticism.** (Some common themes are parenting, Christian lifestyle, women/men, other religious or ethnic groups, political parties).

2. **Renew your mind.** Practice saying, "I'm not the authority over *(fill in the blank)*'s life." Having this mindset disables pride and enables you to use your words to restore and encourage others and not tear them down. (Eph. 4:29).

3. **Behold God's grace and mercy so you can give grace and mercy.** Grace is God giving us what we don't deserve (blessings). Mercy is not giving us what we do deserve, which is punishment for sins. Appreciate the depth of your shortcomings and thank God that His goodness and mercy have followed you all the days of your life (Psalm 23:6).

God, help me to remember Your love and mercy for me. Forgive me for making an idol out of my opinion. I desire to be mindful of my thoughts and the words that flow. Please soften areas of my heart that are not gracious. Help me to not only refrain from criticizing others but myself as well.

Day 8

DESPERATE

Loss of hope; Despair that leads to employing unusual measures to escape the situation.

Trust in the Lord with all your heart, and do no rely on your own understanding; think about Him in all your ways, and He will guide you on the right paths.
PROVERBS 3:5-6

Win at all costs.

The means justifies the end.

By any means necessary.

Desperate times call for desperate measures.

These are sayings used in the face of extreme hardship, but what do they really mean? Lots of people interpret them as a license to do whatever it takes to get what they want. Their justification is that if winning is the goal, then it doesn't matter how you get there. Just get there. I see where they are coming from, but I don't think they count the costs of winning. Although the word desperate is only in one of the phrases, its undertone is apparent in all of them. When I looked up synonyms for desperate, I found words like *frantic, risky, rash,* and *hasty,* which suggests to me that feeling desperate should caution us to slow down, not move full steam ahead.

What about you? How do you see desperation? As you deliberate your position, I'll further explain mine. Think about your goals. I'm sure they are not bad, per se. For instance, it's not sinful to want a promotion at work, to want more money, or to want to get married. The main issue comes up when achieving the goal looks hopeless, and desperation kicks in. We question the effectiveness of our current strategy and create an internal dialogue on why it's okay to employ extreme strategies to meet our goals. This is why paying attention to your emotions is critical because desperation is blinding. Operating in this mode always has a detrimental cost you can't see. Consider this scenario about Rachel, a 34-year-old Christian woman who had been single and celibate for a while.

> Rachel deeply desired to get married and unbeknownst to her, her faith in God secretly diminished after every failed relationship. Consequently, she was unaware that her desire for marriage had turned into a snare. She also didn't realize the desperation she felt when Derrick came along. Derrick seemed like a good guy. He was nice, respectful, and even went to church. Yet, there was this other part of him who believed marriage is "just a piece of paper," and sex within a committed relationship outside of marriage is okay. Derrick was unlike any of the other men Rachel had dated, and she didn't want to lose him over something like celibacy. Out of desperation, Rachel found herself being impatient and compromising her boundaries. She justified her decision to God, herself, and others by claiming Derrick was the "one" for her. All the exterior looked good, but Rachel overlooked the fine print of the interior. Rachel proceeded on in the relationship and pressured Derrick about marriage. She was absolutely thrilled when they got engaged since

God was finally answering her prayers. Needless to say, Rachel was crushed when Derrick broke off the engagement 2 months before the wedding.

Do you see how Rachel's desperation caused her not to discern between good and best? Take a look at your own life. What is that one hopeless situation that makes you feel desperate? These situations are very delicate because your decisions can have painful consequences that far outweigh the pleasure of obtaining your goal. When you feel desperate, the enemy creeps in and says, *"Look around you! This situation won't change. You've got to do something!"* I encourage you to take your eyes off the situation and fix them on God.

Here are 3 truths that have sustained me when I have felt desperate:

a) Remember – God won't withhold anything good from you. (Psalm 84:11)

b) Remember – You cannot fail if you trust in God. (Prov 3:5-6)

c) Remember – You will reap if you faint not. (Gal. 6:9)

God, thank You for the desires of my heart. My deepest desire is (<u>fill in the blank</u>). Forgive me for any ungodly measures I've taken out of desperation. I remind my soul that You can do exceedingly, abundantly, above all that I may ask or think (Eph. 3:20-21). Renew my trust in You and give me the wisdom to know Your hand in my circumstances.

Day 9

DEVASTATED

Overwhelmingly shocked.

Yet He knows the way I have taken; when He has tested me, I will emerge as pure gold.
JOB 23:10

I can easily think of life circumstances that can leave us feeling devastated. The death of a loved one, a medical or mental illness diagnosis, acts of terrorism, a prison sentence, sexual assault, natural disasters, losing your job or home, loved ones who go astray, miscarriage, car wreck, divorce. Even if you've never experienced any of those circumstances, it doesn't mean your emotional reaction is any less. What makes devastation a challenging emotion to conquer is the element of surprise, because your life creed is tested.

From a young age, we are taught the just-world philosophy, which is the belief that life is fair, and people only get what they deserve. Consequently, we believe only good things happen to good people, and bad things happen to bad people. It makes sense that our world is shattered when we encounter something that does not fit this framework. What happens when you're trying your best to live for God, and you still get bad news? It can feel overwhelming and seem unfair.

These situations can lead to a crisis of faith. All kinds of feelings and questions may emerge from feeling devastated, including anger, shame, sadness, and confusion. *Why me, God?* Oh, how I wish I could answer or explain why we experience pain in our lives. What I do know is that our loving, compassionate, and merciful God is not shocked by your devastating situation. He will take you under His wing as you pick up the broken pieces, day by day. God's process of mending us reminds me of the Japanese art of Kintsugi, which means golden joinery. In this beautiful art form, broken and cracked pieces of ceramics are revived by gold dust and lacquer. It is a meticulous process, but the imperfections of the finished pieces make them priceless. Our lives mirror this process, and my prayer is that you will not see your devastation as the end of your life but rather an opportunity for God to refine you into His wondrous masterpiece.

Here are some tips to facilitate your restoration process:

- Steer clear of the temptation to isolate yourself from God and others.
- Acknowledge your feelings of devastation.
- Avoid rushing through the pain.
- Begin to notice the golden lines in the broken pieces of your life.

God, I feel completely devasted because (fill in the blank). I do not understand why this happened to me, but I am thankful that You will never leave me. Help me to draw close to You as I pick up the pieces. Thank you for restoration!

Day 10

DISTRACTED

Difficulty concentrating due to a preoccupied mind.

But each one is tempted when he is carried away and
enticed by his own lust.
JAMES 1:14

In our busy society, there is always something or someone vying for our attention. Our sensory intake is on overload, and we can find it hard to concentrate on what matters most. One of the main patient complaints I hear is, *"Doc, something is wrong with my memory. I think I may have Alzheimer's Disease."* Then I start my spiel about attention and memory, but most of them are not convinced. They figure there must be something wrong because they keep forgetting things, have a hard time focusing, and struggle to complete tasks. They plea for an evaluation and are baffled by the results. Did you know that about 97% of the patients who swear to me they are demented do NOT have a neurocognitive disorder? So, what's the problem? Distraction! That's right, distraction.

I'll show you some of the main sources of distraction that's clouding your mind.

1. *Social Media:* Early in my graduate school days, I was distracted by social media. I would check updates to see what everyone had going on. After I was done, I noticed a shift in my mood as I began to suffer from FOMO (fear of missing

out). I started to feel discontent with the current season of my life. Consequently, I found it hard to concentrate on the tasks and goals for my season.

2. *Sinful Desires:* The Bible says lustful desires draw us away by distracting us and luring us towards sin. Sin is so captivating because it is dangerously fun, exciting, entertaining, and easily occupies our minds.

3. *Busyness:* We are not always distracted by "bad" or sinful things. Our struggles can be brought on by good deeds like helping others, serving in ministry, or productivity in work or school. You might be wondering if this is true, then how can busyness be a distraction. I'll tell you how. Time after time, we get so busy doing and helping others that we neglect self-care or other endeavors God has asked us to do. Too much activity can also distract you from dealing with your inner emotional life.

4. *Psychological Symptoms:* One of the traps of depression and posttraumatic stress disorder (PTSD) is distraction that keeps you focused on or stuck in the past. Similarly, anxiety distracts you by keeping your mind in future mode. These conditions prevent you from being present in the here and now.

After thoughtfully considering this list, do you know who or what has distracted you? Establish a plan of action to reduce interruptions in your mind. Make room in your heart to hear from God.

Father, please keep me in perfect peace as I keep my mind focused on You. Thank You for showing me what things/people/activities are keeping me from hearing from You more clearly.

Day 11

DOUBTFUL

Unsure, uncertain, without faith.

Now if any of you lacks wisdom, he should ask God,
who gives to all generously and without criticizing,
and it will be given to him.
JAMES 1:5

It's okay to admit it. I know as Christians we're supposed to have faith, for without it, it's impossible to please God. I know that James 1:7 says those who doubt should not expect to get anything from the Lord. Yet, the truth is you have doubts, and you feel unsettled or unsure about certain situations. As much as we will and wish for faith, we can silently lose heart when it seems our best efforts and attempts to "just pray about it" are not enough.

I want to remind you that moments of doubt are common for everyone. When I explore the times I've felt doubtful, the circumstances made sense. How could I not doubt when I have prayed for something or someone, and nothing seemed to happen? How could I have faith when the facts just did not add up? It was that very mindset that was the problem. Do you see how I was trying to make sense of what was in front of me (aka *leaning to my own limited understanding*)? What helped me to start tackling doubt was putting James Chapter 1 into context. As much as I know the purpose of trials is to test our faith, I did not realize James was encouraging us to ask God for wisdom when doubt arises during the trials of life (James 1:5). The benefit of walking in wisdom is you get to see the fruit of what the trial produces.

Something else I found useful was talking openly about my doubts to God. Doing so has increased my appreciation and adoration for God because He is so open to hearing me when I feel unsure about situations or even Him. He already knows the contents of our hearts, so telling Him does not come as a surprise. Telling Him is for our healing. There's no topic that's off-limits to God. When I ask others to disclose their doubts, here's the gist of their statements:

> *"I feel doubtful about getting accepted to the program or job. I feel doubtful because my health prognosis does not look good.......because I'm still single. ...because I can't get pregnant ...because my child is acting unruly. ...because I've been praying for change, and it hasn't happened.*

Now, it's your turn to complete the sentence. I feel doubtful because *(fill in the blank)*.

Whew! How did that feel? Even if it felt unnerving, God is compassionate. Remember the story about the boy who had seizures and could not hear or speak? Jesus felt compassion for the boy's father when he admitted his unbelief. Although the request was granted for his son to be healed, the bigger miracle was the removal of his father's doubt (Mark 9:17-27).

Here are some other ways to deal with feelings of doubt.

- Challenge the enemy when he causes you to question your salvation.

- Ask God to reveal if the desires of your heart align with His word and His will.

- Ask God to help you place your focus on His faithfulness and providence and not on what you can visibly see.

- Remind yourself that God is on your side and all things will work together for good because you love Him (Rom. 8:28).

God, thank You for Your open ear to my prayers. I feel doubtful about (fill in the blank). I know Your word is true, so please help my unbelief. Improve my ability to see past my situation to the truth of Your love and compassion for me. Align my desires to the good plans and thoughts You have for me. Give me the wisdom I need to allow this trial to produce the fruit of endurance and increased faith.

Day 12

EMPTY

Without feelings

For what does it benefit a man to gain the
whole world yet lose his life?
MARK 8:36

Do you have a vision for your life? Of course, you do! Go ahead and take a few moments to write down your vision. Like most people, your vision might include having a thriving career, loving family, supportive friends, healthy relationships, good health, and admittedly, some "stuff" too (e.g., fun vacations, comfortable home, nice car, stylish clothes). Now look back over your list and see if some of your vision has already come to fruition. I'm willing to guess there's at least a couple of things that have already manifested. You may have even acquired most of the things on your vision board and did not find the fulfillment you expected. That's where so many people have found themselves but struggle to admit due to fear of judgment or embarrassment. A rich man hides his emptiness because the poor won't understand. A married woman feels guilty about her emptiness when there are so many single women who long to get married. A pastor masks the blankness in his soul because other pastors would love to have his full congregation. Can you relate? You wonder how this can be possible, especially for Christians? The expectation is that Jesus will fill you up, and you will feel content in the midst of actual or perceived lack. Since you're being honest, here. That is not your truth. Your reality is that there's a discontentment and hollowness that shows up in the quiet moments of your life. You try to give yourself pep talks to be more grateful, have more faith, and show up with a smile. Yet, the emotional barrenness seeps back in again.

Feeling empty is tricky because it's hard to describe and pinpoint. For some, it shows up as depression or an inability to experience positive emotions for an extended period of time. For others, it shows up in physical symptoms like a hollowness in their chest or pit in their stomach. However it shows up for you, you just know that something is missing. First, I want to give you permission to acknowledge your feelings of emptiness without any criticism from me. Doesn't that feel good? Now I want to offer a few questions to help you further explore your inner discontentment:

a. **Is your emptiness caused by a lack of identity?** It's natural to go through periods of questioning your identity when you progress through life transitions like graduating from high school/college, entering the dating world, or retirement. The problem comes when the sense of self is chronically absent. This can happen if you were raised in an environment where you never developed a healthy sense of self due to abuse or neglect. It can also occur if you are in a relationship with someone who criticizes your character, and you begin to question your identity.

b. **Whose life are you living?** When you review the vision for your life, consider whether your quests are truly from God. I have encountered numerous people who reach their goal only to confess to me they never wanted to do what they are doing. In an effort to please their parents or maintain the family name, people endeavor to play sports, pursue certain careers, go into ministry, have children, etc. Does this sound like your predicament? When you consider that you might be living someone else's life, doesn't your emptiness now make sense? You may be worried about letting others down if you decide to go in a different direction, and that's understandable. Think about it this way. As much as we are connected, God has still given each of us our own individuality. You might have a talent that is promoted by others, but how much is that support really worth if the price you pay is emptiness? Remember the Parable of the 10 talents (Matt. 25:14-30)? One of the main lessons in the parable is that God will hold us accountable for the stewardship of our abilities, time, and resources. Imagine how fulfilling your life would be if you were to faithfully pursue what God has entrusted to you.

c. **Can you calculate profit and loss?** No, I'm not talking about your financial statement from your bank account. Rather, I'm referring to your emotional statement. We often pursue the dream of owning and stowing possessions, but is it worth it? The accolades we get from others doesn't last. The satisfaction we get soon after we acquire more "stuff" quickly fades, thus leading to the desire for more and more. I want to be clear that owning material possessions is not evil; we have to make sure the possessions do not own us. Our key verse asks us a critical question "For what will it profit a man to gain the whole world and lose his own soul?" The contrast suggests the profit is not worth the loss. Is your emptiness indicative of a lost soul?

Hopefully, seriously examining these 3 questions will shed light on your feelings of emptiness and lead you to lean in to God for answers.

God, my soul feels empty. I need You to fill the void in my heart and help me to pursue the things You want me to pursue that will be truly satisfying.

Day 13

ENVIOUS

Resentful, desirous, covetous.

*For where envy and selfish ambition exist, there is
disorder and every kind of evil.*
JAMES 3:16

*A tranquil heart is life to the body, but jealousy is
rottenness to the bones.*
PROVERBS 14:30

There was a one-of-a-kind study on envy conducted in 2015.
The investigators, N. E. Hinniger and C. R. Harris, examined
who feels envious and what is envied. There were several notewor-
thy findings in the study: 1) Envy is a common emotion experienced by both men and women of all ages, though older adults
were found to envy others less. 2) People are more inclined to
envy people of the same sex and those closer to their age (within 5
years). 3) Younger adults were more likely to envy people based on
perceived attractiveness, academic, social, and romantic relationship success. People of all ages envied career and financial success,
but it was noted that older adults tended to envy those particular
categories more often.

It didn't take this study to show us that envy is a widespread
emotion since we all know that everyone feels it at times. I'm just

thankful the participants in the study were bold enough to report their envy because it's usually shamefully harbored in our hearts. Even though envy is rarely openly discussed, the fact that it's a popular topic searched on the web tells me that we are secretly looking for help in this area. I thought it would be important to include this shameful emotion in the book as it can get us into a lot of trouble if we don't address it head on.

Did you know that jealousy and envy are not the same? We use them interchangeably, but there are subtle differences. Envy is the emotion that comes up when you want what others have, and jealousy is the sentiment that comes up when you fear losing what you already have. As in the study mentioned above, people typically envy things like wealth, material possessions, educational, occupational, and relational status. You want what they have. In contrast, an example of jealousy is if you feel threatened when your best friend starts to spend a lot of time with another friend. You fear losing what you have.

Both jealousy and envy have consequences; they lead to disorder and rot the bones. Nevertheless, it is important to know the difference so you can discern what's in your heart, know how to pray, and know how to respond. When we feel envious of someone else, we have taken our eyes off our own race and determined what God has done for us is insufficient. It also indicates we don't have faith that God has good things in store for us. Instead of responding with genuine praise, we may diminish or one-up the accomplishments of others, be competitive, and feel depressed. When we are jealous, the root emotions are betrayal, fear and insecurity, leading us to respond in suspicious, angry, and controlling ways.

Now that you know the distinction between envy and jealousy, doesn't it explain why God is jealous for our affections? He has rightful ownership of our hearts, and thankfully, He does not respond in controlling ways. Instead, He patiently courts us and waits to show us He can be trusted. I want to impress upon you to be honest with yourself and also take your feelings of envy and jealousy to the Lord. Allow Him to settle your spirit by reminding you that what He has for you is yours, period. You don't want what someone else has because you don't know the price they paid for it or what they have to do to keep it. When you want who and what is uniquely designed by God for you, your feelings of jealousy and envy can be released.

> *Thank You, God, for loving me so much that you don't want to lose me to something or someone who cannot fully love or satisfy me. I am feeling jealous and afraid I will lose (fill in the blank). I pray for a renewed mindset and trust that You are in control of my life.*

> *God, forgive me for measuring someone else's life against my own. Refresh the eyes of my heart to behold the beauty of the gifts and possessions You have given me. I want to genuinely celebrate others without feeling inferior. Help my heart to feel secure in knowing that You will not withhold anything good from me (Psalm 84:11). I will set my affections on You.*

Day 14

FORGOTTEN

To be gone from someone's memory, unremembered

Even if these forget, yet I will not forget you.
ISAIAH 49:15b

L ife goes on and when it does, you can feel forgotten. I hear your thoughts.

What happened to the promises that were made?

How is it that I remember everyone's birthday but mine is recognized after the fact, if at all?

I see pictures of the gathering online with the funny hashtags. Why wasn't I invited?

I was once part of the team, but now it appears anyone barely remembers my name.

Everyone's prayers seem to be getting answered but mine. Has God forgotten me?

I think you'll agree with me that no one wants to be forgotten. I've been there before, so I understand how you are feeling right now. It really hurts to feel forgotten by others we care about or by God. As I journey along, I've realized the importance of perception. How you see it or feel it may not be how it is. When it comes to people, let's try to put some things in perspective by answering a few questions.

Do you notice a pattern of being overlooked in the relationship or is this a one-time incident?

Are you filtering events through the lens of negative beliefs about yourself?

Do you leave room for people to have other friends and tend to other priorities in their lives?

Are you relying too much on one person instead of engaging in self-care and expanding your friendship circle?

These are tough questions, but I believe the answers can shed light on deeper issues and help you cope when you feel forgotten.

When it comes to God, I love how He still speaks even in seasons of perceived silence. He knows what we need before we ask (Matt. 6:8). Check out this message He gave me when I was at a women's conference. During one of the prayer breaks, a dear friend came up to me and said, "God, hasn't forgotten about you." I was appreciative of the word of encouragement but didn't know what led my friend to share that with me. To my knowledge, I didn't feel forgotten. What I didn't realize was that those words were not for that very moment. Rather, it was the reassurance and inspiration I needed for future seasons. God gave that to me before I knew to ask for it and boy, was He right on time! The Holy Spirit has reminded me of those words when I have felt forgotten. It's kept me from giving in to the feelings when they surface.

People will let you down, and even though it's usually unintentional, the pain of feeling forgotten is still real. I acknowledge your feelings of loneliness and isolation. I want to leave you with this truth for today. God remembers you today, and He will never forget you! God even says *"I will not forget you!"* (Isa. 49:15b). He cares about the details of your life, even down to the number of hairs on your head (Luke 12:6-7).

> *God, thank You for loving me enough to make me how*
> *You wanted me. People may forget me, but I'm grateful*
> *that You've never forgotten me. Heal me as I remember*
> *Your love and faithfulness towards me.*

Day 15

GRIEVED

**To be in sorrow or deep distress, especially when
someone passes away.**

Those who mourn are blessed, for they will be comforted.
MATTHEW 5:4

Losing someone you love is a universal experience and one of the most painful feelings in life. Initially, psychological research by Elisabeth Kubler-Ross suggested that grief happens in stages (*denial, anger, bargaining, depression, acceptance*). As more information was gained about the grief process, it was clarified that grief does not happen in a sequential order. Rather, it is a process or cycle in which people experience any variation of the aforementioned components. What does all this mean? It means your grief process is unique and will not look like anyone else's. Because of that reality, there may be times when you believe no one understands exactly how you feel. Even more surprising is when you don't react in the way you expect either. I'll let you in on a piece of my grief journey after losing my mother.

I quietly cared for my mother for 8 years before she passed away. My spiritual intuition and experience working in a medical setting gave me cues that her time here on earth was drawing near. Despite all my skills and experience caring for others, including working on a hospice unit, I was still not prepared for the horror of seeing my mother's lifeless body in front of me as we sat alone in her room. I collapsed on the floor and wailed! In one last breath, my life would forever be changed. As of writing this book, it has been a little over a year, and the emotions are still fresh. In my reflection, I can see aspects of my grief process that are exactly how others told me it would be and others that are not that way at all. There are days when I know what stage of grief I'm in and other days when I just know I'm hurting. What I do know is that God has been there every step of the way.

In addition to grieving the death of a loved one, one could also grieve the loss of relationships, dreams, and roles. For example, a couple can experience deep sorrow when they accept that they are biologically unable to have children. As such, the couple will likely have to mourn the loss of the dream they had in mind. Another example is when people go through divorce. They are apt to feel an emptiness or sorrow for the lost role of being a husband or wife. It makes sense that grief is part of the transition since they have lost a piece of their identity from that phase of life.

One thing that makes grief so hard to process is the fact that your mind and heart are suspended with time, yet life goes on. The caring calls and texts stop, and you're left to figure this thing out. A major part of my healing has been in my remembering Jesus' humanity. When Jesus wept over Lazarus' death, I was reminded that He has compassion for my grief (John 11:35). Yes, Jesus knew He would raise Lazarus from the dead, but His tears before doing so helped me to know He empathizes with my pain. So, in your grief process, I encourage you to remember Jesus' humanity along with His divine nature. Receive God's comfort for you and be open to the ways He leads others to comfort you.

You may also find these other tips profitable as you process your loss:

- Take all the time you need and don't rush the grieving process.

- Don't avoid grieving by masking your emotions.

- Be patient when others try to comfort you.

God, thank You for the life of my loved one and for keeping him/her in Your presence. I am deeply saddened about the loss. As I grow through the healing journey, may I find peace in knowing that I grieve with hope.

Day 16

GUILTY

**Remorseful; Feeling responsible for a
perceived wrongdoing or error.**

*There is therefore now no condemnation to them which
are in Christ Jesus, who walk not after the flesh, but after
the Spirit.*
ROMANS 8:1 (KJV)

*I cheated on my spouse. I am a horrible parent. I am a murderer. I allowed myself to be raped. I had sex before marriage. I said something
I should not have said. I am a poor leader.*

Can you guess the question that prompted these answers? You're
right. *Why do you feel guilty?* I'm curious about how you would
answer that question. Whether your answer includes any or none
of those statements, we can all identify with feeling guilty. I'll share
something I learned about guilt in my professional life that has been
so helpful in my personal life. Guilt is a feeling that occurs when we
have done something inconsistent with our values and standards.
Guilt and shame are close cousins, so when one is present, the other
is usually nearby. When shame creeps in, you start associating your
identity with your behavior (e.g., I made a mistake, so I am a mistake.) The best part of what I learned is the need to look more closely
at intent because that determines the validity of guilt. If your actions

resulted in an intended outcome, guilt is warranted. If not, regret is a more appropriate and healthy emotion.

Knowing the difference between guilt and regret helps you to assign emotions appropriately. Trust me when I tell you Satan, our enemy knows the difference. He's our accuser and loves to keep our mistakes on repeat so we can mistake our behavior for our identity. He wants to keep you feeling condemned and ashamed. Praise God there is now, therefore, NO condemnation for those who are in Christ (see key verse).

If you're like any of the people I've asked before, you're thinking I don't understand the severity of your situation. You want to convince me that your guilt is warranted. You believe the mistake you made was unthinkable. You're not quite sure you deserve to release the guilt, but stay with me for a bit longer. Although you can assume that feeling guilty is the price you need to pay for your choices, I'd like for you to get a fuller picture of what guilt does to you. It leads to ruminating on the past, rehearsing negative self-talk, avoiding others and God, engaging in self-harm, displaying anger and violence towards others, inability to tolerate constructive feedback, and being unforgiving of yourself and others. So, you're right. I don't know all the details of your situation, but I still have good news for you! Whatever you did or did not do, Jesus' love covers it. He does not constantly remind us of our mistakes (Psalm 103:12). Jesus paid the ultimate price for our sins…ALL of them…even the one you think is unforgivable. The price of guilt costs way too much. Trade it in for Christ's compassion and self-compassion.

God, thank You that I don't have to carry around the burden of guilt any longer. Help me to be a sheep who hears Your voice when you want me to change my behavior or thoughts. I cast out any thoughts that keep me feeling guilty, and I receive the gift of Your grace and forgiveness.

DAY 17

HATEFUL

Feelings of intense hostility, dislike, contempt.

*Then said Jesus, Father, forgive them; for
they know not what they do.*
LUKE 23:34

Curiously, hatred was the last emotion I identified for this book. It was not on my original list, but when the Holy Spirit brought it to my attention, I knew it could not be omitted. I dreaded writing about it because it's such a heavy and uncomfortable topic. We're taught that it's an ugly word, so who wants to admit they feel hatred? Yet, the reality is that many people harbor hatred in their hearts. This realization was stirred to the surface when a court case in my hometown of Dallas, Texas made national news. If the verdict itself wasn't divisive enough, the sentencing and its aftermath were outright disruptive to the consciousness of many, especially Christians. It caused countless people, including myself to take a long, hard look at the contents of our hearts.

Counseling people who feel hateful and those who are hated has provided me a unique perspective on the matter. These delicate encounters have led to my asking 2 crucial questions:

Picture the father of a son whose murderer was acquitted or handed down a seemingly light sentence. Picture the husband whose wife got pregnant by another man or the woman who was raped and then dismissed as being promiscuous. Picture the son who was repeatedly beaten by his stepfather or the couple on the receiving end of a racial slur. Picture the families of victims killed in hate crimes. *Do they have a legitimate right to feel hatred towards those who transgressed against them?*

To answer this question, I was reminded of Jesus as He hung on the cross. In His agony, He said, "Father, forgive them; for they know not what they do" (Luke 23:34 KJV). What incredible strength and discernment! He looked beyond the actions of those who crucified Him and saw their hearts. This is a great illustration of how we should handle the heinous offenses that come into our lives or the lives of our loved ones. Ask God to forgive them and truly bless their hearts. As Christians, we don't have a right to hate others even if they hate us.

Now let us flip to the other side and look at my second question. *What do ethnic minorities and ethnic majorities, rich and poor, homosexual and heterosexual, Republican and Democrat, American citizens and illegal immigrants, educated and uneducated, Christians and Muslims, police officers, women who've had abortions, ex-convicts, and drug addicts ALL have in common?* You guessed it. Emotions!

When we keep this awareness at the forefront of our hearts, we can remember that emotions are the fabric of our human connectedness and keep our judgements in godly perspective. We cannot utilize God's Word to justify our hatred. While God calls us to "hate" sin, He does not permit us to sit on His throne and condemn others.

When we are tempted to hold on to feeling hatred, we should contemplate the negative outcomes:

- It separates us from one another and limits our social and emotional support network (Prov. 10:12 KJV).

- It hinders our prayers because we are harboring unforgiveness (Mark 11:25-26).

- It blocks peace and productivity because our minds become consumed with ruminating about others (Phil. 4:8).

- It decreases our empathy for others.

- It becomes contagious to others who look to us for influence.

- It poisons our speech (Eph. 4:29).

Maybe you don't hate a particular group of people, but you hate a particular person who hurt you or someone you love. My prayer is for you to dig up hatred and replace it with love. This won't be an overnight process, so be patient with yourself as you work through this rough heart work. Reconciliation may not always be possible or desirable, but love in our hearts is always an option.

God, grant me the serenity to accept the people I cannot change, the courage to change the one I can, and the wisdom to know it's me. – Author unknown

Day 18

HOPELESS

Without hope of improvement.

Happy is the one whose help is the God of Jacob, whose hope is in the Lord his God.
PSALM 146:5

Just 8 months ago, Carter's life was thriving. He was an executive at a top healthcare firm, and he worked a paid part-time position in ministry at the church. His marriage to Tessa was progressing along peacefully and their 2 children were happy. Although he was unexpectedly laid off, he had faith that he could easily find another job given his experience. Well, his certainty was dwindling each time he got a rejection email after a job interview. He just got another one today. To make matters worse, his ministry position dissolved due to budget cuts, and his father's diagnosis of prostate cancer was confirmed. At least, he still had the support of his wife, so he decided to talk to her so they could brainstorm a strategy for next month's bills. To his surprise, Tessa told him she was unhappy and wanted a divorce. She refused his offer for couple's counseling and said she and the children would be moving with her parents immediately. With a series of disappointments, Carter felt hopeless.

Can you connect with Carter's pain? We all know life has disappointments and though difficult, we seem to be able to bounce back from them. I attribute that to the fact that we have some other thriving areas of our lives to offset the weight of the unpleasurable situation. Despite the disappointment, we still tend to have an overall positive outlook on the future. This viewpoint helps us to remain determined to see and make progress. But when there's one setback after the other? That takes disappointment to a whole new level as it's a much deeper pain to heal and a darker path to navigate. You have to battle the belief that your resources have dried up. No more money, opportunities, available partners, medication, time, energy, patience, health, and the list goes on and on. Essentially, your confidence is gone, and no amount of inspiration can penetrate the despair. Once hopelessness sets in, people make decisions based on what they see right now. Unlike desperation, which compels you to take action, hopelessness repels you from doing anything.

Maybe you've been praying about, thinking about, talking about, and dreaming about something that has not yet happened. Have you been hoping for employment, addiction recovery, a spouse, increased finances, improved medical or mental health prognosis, children, friends, wayward family, and it seems that things are getting worse? I don't know the exact circumstances that have triggered your feelings of hopelessness, but I want to assure you there is always hope when you put your hope in the Lord. Often, we put hope in our skills, family, friends, social connections, beauty, money, education, wisdom, and knowledge. When we do that, it's no wonder we feel hopeless because those things and people are limited resources. God is our source, and His resources are unlimited. Our key verse tells us there is a blessing attached to putting our hope in the Lord. Our mood is restored because it's not contingent upon external circumstances. How can you renew your hope in God today?

God, thank You for bringing me to this place in my life so I can learn a different part of Your character. I am feeling hopeless about my circumstances, but I want to put my hope in You alone. Show me the areas of my life I need to surrender to You. Please restore the joy of my salvation as I wait for the blessings attached to putting my hope in You.

DAY 19

IGNORED

Disregarded and unacknowledged.

You will call to Me and come and pray to Me,
and I will listen to you.
JEREMIAH 29:12

I'm sitting there waiting for a response to a call, text, or email. Initially, I try to remain hopeful and gracious, but eventually reality sets in. I'm being ignored. I wonder if you've ever been there. We attempt to understand it better by recalling our last interactions. We wonder if we said or did anything to warrant such behavior. Sometimes we even go so far as to reaching out again and feel even worse when we're ignored again. You begin to ask, *"Do they care? Am I that unimportant? Did I do something wrong?"*

What makes being ignored more frustrating is the assumption that the disregard is intentional. It implies the person saw or heard you but willfully chose not to reply. To ease this sentiment, we need to put some things into perspective as it pertains to our human relationships:

1. **Know the nature and quality of the relationship.** If you know the person to otherwise be responsive, there might be a logical explanation for their unresponsiveness.

2. **Adjust your expectations.** Some answers require time and thoughtfulness.

3. **Readjust your focus.** The more we focus on something, the stronger the intensity. Are there self-care activities you can engage in to manage your frustrations? Are there other relationships you can cultivate?

If we're honest, we may even have similar questions when God seemingly does not answer prayers. *"Does God hear me? Does He care? Does God really exist?"* When you feel ignored by God, we can apply those same considerations to our relationship with Him:

1. **Know the nature of your relationship with God.** He loves and cares for us. The Word assures us that He listens to our prayers (Jer. 29:12). He is the ultimate authority, so He has Divine reasons to delay your answers.

2. **Adjust your expectations.** Do you expect that God answers every prayer, including requests that are not in His will? Do you demand Him to immediately tell you the answer before giving you time to apply what He's already told or taught you?

3. **Readjust your focus.** Have you been so focused on the response from this one area in your life that other areas of your life are ignored or disobeyed?

God, thank You for comforting me when I feel ignored by people. Help me to have the proper perspective on my relationships with others. I ask for wisdom and courage to separate myself from those whose hearts are not pure towards me. I'm grateful that You never ignore me, but love me enough to strengthen me with silence, when needed. Help me to be more eager to hear from You.

DAY 20

IMPATIENT

Anxious, hasty, unwilling to wait.

*A prudent person with insight foresees danger coming
and prepares himself for it. But the senseless rush blindly
forward and suffer the consequences.*
PROVERBS 22:3 (TPT).

L ife is full of opportunities to wait. Waiting in line, airport lay-
overs, traffic, waiting for answered prayers, waiting on hold,
waiting for children to be born, waiting for children to become
adults, waiting at the doctor's office. Wait! Wait! Wait! Maybe this
explains why there are so many articles, books, and sermons about
waiting on God. Even though I have benefitted from a number of
these resources, I noticed they mainly focus on reasons God may
want us to wait, such as He is working to develop patience in us, He's
preparing the blessing itself, or what we have asked for is not in His
will. However, I have not found many resources that explore why we
might be impatient in the first place. In my prayer time and research,
I realized one of the biggest reasons for impatience is pride. The rest
of what we see is the fruit of it. Pride causes us to have unrealistic
expectations of ourselves, others, and God. Let's say you're learning a
new skill at work. Pride says, *"I shouldn't make mistakes"* and causes
you to beat yourself up when your learning takes longer than expected. What about when someone is moving slowly in line at the store?

Pride says, *"My time is more important than other people's time"* and causes you to be rude with the clerk when it's your turn. A more personal illustration is when a close family member does not make the decisions you want them to make. Pride says, *"My way is better"* and leads you to interact in ungodly ways.

Impatience has a propensity to creep into our relationship with God. We often assume that our Christian deeds and goodness makes us more deserving of getting high-speed answers to prayers. Pride says, *"I shouldn't have to wait because my service to God has earned me a "skip the line" bracelet."* Consequently, we end up making poor decisions that lead to God's permissive will rather than His divine will. What's the difference, you ask? God will permit us to make our own decisions at any time, even ones that are not in His plan for us (permissive will). These choices may initially ease the discomfort of waiting, but they eventually lead to additional suffering and sends us back to God's waiting room. In contrast, waiting for God's divine plan will feel uncomfortable upfront, but results in the fruit of peace and assuredness of His promises.

A big lesson I learned on waiting came when I was in the process of building my home. I was so ready to see the foundation laid as that meant my house would be well on its way to being built. My family and I drove by frequently to see what looked like nothing being done. It was just a mound of dirt and then several piles of dirt. Still no foundation. What was taking them so long?! What I didn't know was that laying the foundation was actually not the first step as I'd assumed. I didn't understand so much had to be considered and completed before the foundation was laid. The land had to be prepped and certain structures put in place to support the foundation. Oooh, now I see. Looking back, what if I'd tried to go and help them by pouring the foundation myself? What if my impatience led me to pull the contract because I deemed the builders to be incompetent and inefficient? What if pride led me to demand the contractors skip steps (because my way was better) and complete the construction earlier than planned? My home would have been cosmetically nice for a moment but crumbling as soon as the weather changed. I'm glad I waited on God's divine plan.

The process of constructing my home mirrors our life in that it initially appears God is doing nothing and needs our assistance to hurry the progress along. However, I assure you that God is *always* at work, and His timing is *always* best. Years ago, I read *Calm My Anxious Heart by Linda Dillow)* and it was life-changing for me. There was one profound quote from the book that stuck with me, *"Happiness is getting what we want; contentment is wanting what we get."* Isn't that powerful? When you learn contentment, it forces pride out of the equation, and impatience soon follows.

If you're struggling with impatience, here are some strategies you can use while you're waiting.

- **Take care of your physical and mental health**. When we are emotionally or physically fatigued, it is hard to embrace the spiritual discipline of waiting well.

- **Strengthen your spiritual muscles to weaken your fleshly desires.** You can do this by studying the list in Galatians 5:19-21 to see if any of those activities or attitudes are feeding your impatience.

- **Take stock of what impatience has cost you.** Has it led to poor decisions, financial problems, poor quality relationships, unstable mood, poor reputation or low self-image?

All in all, what I'm saying is that impatience has a price. Are you willing to pay?

> *God, thank You for Your patience with me. I ask for forgiveness for not trusting Your timing in answering my prayers. Renew me emotionally and physically so I may produce the spiritual fruit of patience. I want to exchange unbelief and pride for contentment and patience. Please help me to learn to wait well.*

Day 21

INCOMPETENT

Unqualified, unskilled, lacking ability.

And God is able to make every grace overflow to you, so
that in every way, always having everything you need,
you may excel in every good work.
2 CORINTHIANS 9:8

Early on in my doctoral training, I was talking to my cousin about
how advanced students and professors in my school program
were smart. Unexpectedly, she commented, "You're smart too." Her
comment gave me pause to realize I was admiring them to the point
where I implied that I was not capable of being "on that level." I felt
incompetent. When was the last time you felt that way?

If you're not sure, let me clarify by noting that incompetence is
not the same as humility. There is a difference between recognizing
the need for more training and experience in an area and a pervasive
spirit of incompetence. In the former, there is a willingness to learn,
ask questions, be vulnerable and take appropriate risks to gather necessary skills for your assignment. In the latter, there is a timidity that
is present due to negative self-talk that prevents you from growing.

The good news is that we can learn from Moses, who led the people away from Pharaoh (see Exodus Chapters 3-4). When God called
Moses to the task, he easily gave God a list of his inadequacies (i.e.,

I'm not good enough. I don't have a big enough reputation for them to trust me (aka social media following)). I appreciate Moses' honesty by telling God he felt unqualified and unprepared for the task. What I love even more is God's comforting responses as a Father to Moses. God assured Moses He would equip him for the job.

You're probably wondering how I overcame feeling incompetent. Like Moses, I told God my inadequacies and began to put things in a proper perspective. It was not fair or wise for me to compare myself to people who already had the experience I had yet to gain. God equipped me, and He is still equipping me for each assignment I face. Maybe you've just been promoted at work or want to apply for a new job. Maybe you feel incompetent to be a godly parent or spouse. You may even feel incompetent to lead your church or small group. I hope our key verse inspires you to give God your list and watch His grace abound to you so you can excel in every good work.

God, right now, I feel so inadequate and worry I can't do the task at hand. I am leaning on You for the wisdom, skills, knowledge, and boldness for this season. Remove any unhealthy comparison that feeds my feelings of inadequacy.

Day 22

INSECURE

Uncertain, lacking confidence.

*For it is God which worketh in you both to will
and to do of his good pleasure.*
PHILIPPIANS 2:13 (KJV)

In an age where social media promotes the fallacy of always winning, overnight celebrity, daily success, flawless bodies, perfect marriages and kids, everyday vacations, it's no wonder that insecurities are at an all-time high. Even if we're not influenced by social media, none of us are exempt from feeling insecure as we all lack confidence in some areas of our lives. Some of the leading categories of insecurities are below:

- Physical (e.g., *My body doesn't look attractive enough.*)
- Social (e.g., *My circle of friends is not influential enough.*)
- Intellectual (e.g., *I'm not smart enough.*)
- Financial (e.g., *I don't make enough money.*)
- Relational (e.g., *I'm single/divorced, so something must be wrong with me.*)
- Spiritual (e.g., *My spiritual gifts aren't as good as others' gifts.*)

Do your inner thoughts sound like these examples? You are certainly not alone in your insecurities, as none of us are exempt. Did you know that even the most confident person you know or admire has insecurities? That's right! Fret not. There are a couple of ways we can use insecurities to our advantage to reduce its impact on our lives.

First, get to the root of why you feel insecure by exploring the nature and quality of your past and current relationships. Maybe you grew up in a critical environment, so someone else's voice became your voice. Maybe you are in an unhealthy relationship, and your partner makes judgmental comments, or perhaps someone you love abandoned you. Maybe you have adopted someone else's poor behavior as your identity or responsibility. As soon as you have a better grasp in this area, you can start to challenge your thoughts.

Second, find out if you lack true identity, which leads to a false sense of purpose and security. One of the main prayer requests I get is for help finding purpose. How I long for everyone to find his/her purpose. It brings about so much fulfillment and security. Without it, it's easy to fall prey to comparisons. You start to look for your identity in other people, which is dangerous. Some people have identified their purpose but have not yet started walking in it. This is a slippery slope too, because the root still leads to insecurity. Everyone harps on *finding your why.* I say it's more critical to find out *who* you are so you can find your what, why, and how.

Before we move on, I'd like for you to try this simple, yet thought-provoking exercise by completing this sentence.

When I become (fill in the blank) enough, I will have more confidence.

If you filled in the blank with anything other than increased identity in the Lord, the other things on your list will deceive you. Insecurities die hard. Have you ever noticed a different insecurity pops up like the children's whack-a-mole game as soon as you have obtained certain goals? That is because only confidence in the Lord is lasting and satisfying.

Once you get to the root of your insecurity, you can better understand how it manifests in your life. For some, it manifests as arrogance, control, perfectionism, and over achievement, whereas, for others, it shows up as low self-esteem, jealousy, timidity, and lack of productivity. To be clear, insecurity is not the same concept as humility. With humility, you recognize your growth edges, but you remain confident in Christ's ability to equip you for the season or situation in which you're in.

No matter how your insecurities manifest, I encourage you to turn them into character development opportunities. Instead of beholding all the goodness in others, spend time appreciating the goodness in your own virtues. Instead of avoiding certain opportunities or permitting those insecurities to lead you to engage in unhealthy behaviors, try something new and healthy. Use those moments as a chance to capture a different part of God's character. Let Him shape you and your desires to do His good purposes.

Remember this: God wants you to be confident, but in Him. Even when seasons of doubt arise, you will remain planted like a tree near water, and you will also continue producing fruit (Jer. 17:8).

*God, thank You for helping me find confidence in You.
Help me to be satisfied with the gifts You placed in me
and to find and walk in Your purpose for my life. I
thank You for working in me to will and to do Your good
pleasure (Phil. 2:13 KJV).*

Day 23

IRRITABLE

Easily provoked to annoyance or anger.

Love is not ill-mannered or selfish or irritable.
I CORINTHIANS 13:5a (GNT)

If I were to ask what's bugging you, I'm sure you could easily come up with a list of things and people who irritate you. Your list might include familiar irritants such as waiting in line longer than expected, having your order placed incorrectly, being inconvenienced, the know-it-all coworker, your favorite sports team losing the game on a technicality, the nosy neighbor, or being disturbed while sleep or working intently on a task. Everyone feels irritated at times, and usually it's short-lived and infrequent. Irritability becomes an issue when it's a pervasive emotion that interferes with your daily life. In my community, there's a phrase for the person who is constantly or easily irritated, 'bad nerves.' It means the person is more than irritable on occasion. They are prickly, impatient, and crochety all the time and they are particularly hard to get along with. Feeling irritable is normal, but it's how we express it that contributes to being known as the person with "bad nerves."

After feeling irritable for a long time, you are probably no longer aware of your mood and how you come across to others. Here's your litmus test: Do you frequently have to apologize for how you reacted? Do people avoid you or seem hesitant to approach you? Are you easily triggered? If you answered yes to these questions, you may be the sleeping mama or papa bear no one wants to poke.

If you are struggling in this area of your emotional life, there's hope. Go through this checklist to start the process of undoing your irritability:

- ✓ **Identify the source of your irritation.** Do you have untreated trauma, depression, or anxiety, or an untreated medical condition? Are you suffering from side effects of medication? Are you getting enough rest and proper nutrition?

- ✓ **Name your triggers.** Irritation is like the low grumblings that you hear before the volcano erupts. When you know your triggers, you can catch irritation before it turns to anger.

- ✓ **Transform your mood with gratitude.** Irritability is generally the result of circumstances not going the way we want them to go. Challenge yourself to be thankful in all things (I Thess. 5:18). I can't imagine being easily provoked when my heart is glad and thankful.

- ✓ **Learn to love God's way.** The Word tells us that love is not irritable, so we have to work hard to be compassionate and extend grace to ourselves and others when expectations are not met (I Cor. 13:4-5).

- ✓ **Get a new outfit.** Clothe yourself with compassion, kindness, humility, gentleness, and patience (Col. 3:12).

What can you check off your list today?

Dear God, thank You for bringing my irritability to my awareness. I need your grace and strength to learn to respond calmly. Thank You for settling my spirit and helping me to restore my interactions with others.

Day 24

LONELY

Feeling emotionally isolated, lacking companionship.

He will not leave you or forsake you.
DEUTERONOMY 31:6

Loneliness is a natural emotion we have all experienced, but when it's a pervasive feeling, it can be discouraging and make life feel dull. Loneliness is not to be confused with being alone, which refers to your state of being in which no one is physically with you. Although society shuns being alone and has assigned it a negative connotation, it is not a bad thing. Unfortunately, our individualistic culture has become artificially collectivistic. This means our society judges people based on social status and connections even if they are not authentic (i.e., marital status, # of kids, network, church congregation size, social media followers, etc.). When we get caught in that dissatisfying race, we can end up feeling lonely. When I analyze the times I've felt lonely, they fall into 3 basic categories.

1. *Natural Disconnection* – This is an expected emotional response to the end of or loss of a meaningful relationship like a death or break up.

2. *Spiritual Disconnection* – This is an internal alarm that goes off when I have not spent quality time with the Lord.

3. *Social Disconnection* – This is a feeling that happens when I have been intentionally or unintentionally disconnected from others who refresh my mood and spirit.

Each of those categories provide valuable information about what action steps I need to take when I feel lonely. For instance, when I recognize my feeling lonely is due to longing for my late mother, I grant myself space to grieve and mourn. When I have been socially connected but still feel lonely, it's a chance that I am spending time with people who are not purposed to be in my life in that season or at all. It may mean that I have been shutting people out who belong in my life. What I have to do is stop and appraise the quality and fruit of my relationships. Most importantly, when I feel lonely due to spiritual disconnection, that is my clue that I have not spent as much time with God to fill that area of my life. I have to unplug and spend time with Him.

God designed us to need and want relationships and feel known, but He is the ultimate satisfier of our loneliness. This truth is seen in one of my favorite stories in the Bible, the Samaritan woman at the well (John 4:1-29). I love how Jesus knew her so intimately that He recognized all the things she had done to fill the void in her heart. Yet, He did not judge her and invited her to talk to Him openly and honestly. Although this is a popular Bible story, what is often overlooked is the fact that she left her water jar at the well. I believe that was symbolic of internal fulfillment after her intimate encounter with the Lord. Like this woman, our loneliness can cause us to do things that are not fulfilling in the long run. I'm sure you've been there before too. What has loneliness caused you to do or not do? I invite you to explore the source(s) of your loneliness and find ways to get reconnected.

God, thank You that You would never leave me nor forsake me. Help me to overcome my loneliness by connecting with You and others who are beneficial for my emotional and spiritual health. Please give me the strength to draw closer to You and be okay with knowing I am set apart for a purpose.

Day 25

LOST

Off course, adrift, unable to be found.

If a man has 100 sheep, and one of them goes astray,
won't he leave the 99 on the hillside and go and search
for the stray? In the same way, it is not the will of your
Father in heaven that one of these little ones perish.
MATTHEW 18:12;14

Take a mental car ride with me as I recall my journey to a place I had never been. I was driving along the highway, and the GPS was guiding me to my destination. As I listened to the instructions and observed my surroundings, I drew 2 conclusions. Either this was the long route, or I was completely lost. As such, I decided to take my own route only to get further down the road to ask myself, *"Where am I? How did I get here?"* Can you relate to my predicament of feeling lost?

There's something very unsettling about feeling lost because the longer you feel that way, the more panic and hopelessness sets in. In my work, I have encountered people who feel lost in their singleness, marriage, career, and ministry, and they yearn to get their internal compass recalibrated. You might be in a relationship now and feel lost. Perhaps there has been a big change in your life, and your roles have changed. Maybe an addiction has caused you to lose yourself.

Perhaps sin has led you away from your relationship with God. Maybe you never knew your purpose in life, so you have pursued things and people to feel worthy. Feelings of guilt, shame, or pride can prevent you from reaching out for direction when you feel lost. This is a great place for the enemy to trap you so he can whisper lies to you like, *"God is mad at you. You need to fix this on your own before you can go back to Him."* When the enemy has your ear, he can offer you solutions that will keep you off course and away from God's plans for you.

I find it so comforting to marvel at the parable of the lost sheep (Luke 15:1-7). Like any good shepherd, Jesus lovingly pursues me. He eagerly leaves 99 sheep to go find the 1 lost sheep (me). I know He'll readily pursue you, too. As you find your way to a full and meaningful life, I challenge you to:

- Return to God's blueprint (His Word) to seek direction.
- Ask God for His plans for you.
- Allow God to direct your paths by trusting and consulting Him in every area of your life (Prov. 3:5-6).

God, thank You for knowing me intimately before I was born. Thank You for making me unique for a special purpose. Forgive me for looking up to other things and people (including myself) to find my worth and direction. Strengthen me to forgive myself and see myself the way You see me, so I can pursue and accept opportunities and relationships that are aligned with my purpose and decline all others. Thank You for welcoming me with open arms.

Day 26

MISUNDERSTOOD

Misconceived, misinterpreted, mistaken.

*Let us search out and examine our ways, and turn back
to the Lord.*
LAMENTATIONS 3:40

One of my struggles is feeling misunderstood. I guess it's because I want to believe I am a great communicator. What do you know about effective communicators? At a minimum, they are genuine, and they listen. They ask questions, and they convey their message in a direct and concise manner. When someone misunderstands me, I think I can clarify and justify myself enough that it will easily clear up any misinterpretation. I have all these skills, so what's the problem? Life is much more complex than applying good communication skills. I'll mention a few incidents that lead me to this realization.

- A few of my family members assumed and then spread the rumor that I'd conceived a baby by a married man. (*Ouch!*)

- Many people have discounted my input because they assume everything I know was learned through my education. (*If they only knew what I've been through along the way.*)

- On several occasions, my problems have been minimized as people mistakenly presume my career has taught me all the answers. (*I wish it were that easy.*)

How would you have handled those situations? My initial instinct was to explain myself because that would help people see me how I see myself, right? Not necessarily so. Sadly, there were times I got caught in a cycle of explaining, feeling frustrated, explaining again, and feeling further mistaken. At other times, I couldn't provide more details and had to sit with feeling misunderstood. As I matured, it hit me there are more factors at play than simply trying to explain my position.

Most importantly, I have to appraise the prevailing spirit at work in the misunderstanding. Does the person genuinely want to come to an understanding with me, or are they determined to proceed in their own mindset? In other words, is this person's goal to edify or condemn me? Another major factor to consider is my own behavior. Lamentations 3:40 tells us to examine our ways. When I feel misunderstood, I must seriously consider whether my own words or behavior contributed to others having the wrong impression of me. I'm not implying that I change my behavior every time someone misreads me. I'm merely suggesting that I try to look at things from a different angle.

Knowing the answer to those major questions helps me determine my response, if a response is even warranted. Sometimes, responding does not help the situation. God is showing me how to navigate this area of human interaction. Not everything needs to be addressed. It takes a great amount of strength not to react to every misunderstanding. For those who already have an opinion of me settled in their mind, I have had to find peace in knowing myself in God rather than expending emotional energy trying to correct their perception of me.

Do you find yourself struggling with feeling misunderstood? Despite what you may think, you can learn to tolerate feeling misunderstood. Remember, God knows you intimately, and Jesus understands how you feel because He, too, was misunderstood.

God, thank You for knowing and understanding me
(Psalm 139:2). Help me discern which matters of
misunderstanding I can amend and which I cannot.
I need Your strength to see that I don't have to be
emotionally impacted or controlled by what
others think of me.

Day 27

NUMB

Without feeling or sensation.

Restore the joy of Your salvation to me,
and give me a willing spirit.
PSALM 51:12

Have you or anyone you know ever gone under anesthesia for a procedure? Thankfully, I have not had any major surgeries, but I can readily recall the time I had all my wisdom teeth extracted many years ago. I was so nervous, and I voiced it to the doctor when he asked how I was feeling before the procedure. I said, *"I'm scared I might feel everything during the surgery."* The doctor soothed my fears when he smiled and said, *"I promise you won't feel a thing."* That was a bold promise, but you know what? I didn't feel a thing.

Anesthesia still amazes me. It's a temporary loss of (physical) sensation that is medically-induced, so a person does not feel the pain of a surgical procedure. Although this is a useful practice, would anyone want to be in this state long after the procedure is over? I think not. Well, this discomfort is similar to the emotional numbness that many people encounter long after painful psychological experiences.

There seem to be a couple of ways numbness comes about. One of the ways is when a person experiences so much emotional distress from single or multiple events, that she eventually becomes numb to additional painful experiences. It's like their emotional circuit breaker is fried from overload and the emotions shut themselves off for protection. Another way that emotional numbness comes about is when a person has experienced so much emotional distress that he intentionally engages in behavior and activities to shut off the pain (e.g. overeating, godless sex, substances, exercise, busyness, etc.). In a nutshell, emotional numbness can be voluntary or involuntary and offers respite when emotions are too much to handle. Our nature is to avoid pain, so it's understandable that it sometimes seems easier not to feel any emotions at all.

Whenever someone feels numb, I've found it useful to walk them through the exercise of making a list of pros and cons of remaining that way.

PROS	CONS
-I don't have to feel pain right now.	*-I don't ever address the root of my psychological pain.*
	-I don't get to experience the fullness of positive emotions like joy and peace.
	-My relationships with God and others are not as close as they could be.
	-I engage in risky behavior to feel anything at all (i.e., cutting, excessive tattooing, reckless driving).

Each time I've done this exercise with people, they can only find one perceived benefit to feeling numb. Can you come up with any other pros? Looking at this list probably brings up the next natural question. *What if I start to feel emotions, and I can't handle them, or I can't turn them off?* Rest assured that no one cries forever and God's Word tells us it will eventually pass (Psalm 30:5).

These 2 tips can accompany you on your journey as you begin to feel again.

1. Acknowledge the pain to yourself, God, and others who are safe.

2. Seek support from a pastor, trusted friend/family member, or mental health professional.

Remember: God wants you to experience the (full) joy of your salvation.

God, I am deeply hurting, but my heart has hardened
to the pain. Hold my hand as I begin to feel again.
Thank You for healing the areas of my life that have been
desensitized and bringing forth beauty for ashes.

Day 28

OFFENDED

Hurt, resentful, upset, or angry by what is said or done.

A person's insight gives him patience, and his
virtue is to overlook an offense.
PROVERBS 19:11

If there is one thing that gives me an opportunity to apply every Scripture I've learned, it is offense. I mean Jesus assures us offenses will certainly come, so I don't understand why am I surprised, hurt, or upset when they occur. In most situations, you feel better prepared when you know something is coming. Not with offense. There must be something about it that makes them hard to navigate. Let's take a look.

In psychology, we have this very interesting concept called Fundamental Attribution Error (FAE), which is our tendency to blame someone's behavior on internal factors. Alternatively, we are more likely to justify our own behavior with external factors. To show you what I mean, picture how you would respond to this scenario:

A close friend of yours has been raving about his new friend, Brian. Your friend said he could not wait to introduce the two of you at an upcoming dinner party. You're all geared up to meet Brian, and when you finally do, all you get is a fist bump and a barely audible 'hello.'

What is your initial impression of Brian? My guess is you probably think Brian is arrogant, standoffish, and disinterested, which upholds the FAE. Your first impression is not likely to consider that Brian may not be feeling well, or he could have just gotten disturbing news before the party.

Why is FAE important? I see it as a major contributor to our feeling offended. We do not afford people the same grace we would want extended to us. We want people to consider our circumstances before making a judgement about our character, but we are not quick to do the same for others. God wants us to do unto others as we would have them do unto us (Luke 6:31).

Now, I realize FAE does not explain away all offenses or immediately soothe them, so I put together a list of other factors to keep in mind when you feel offended.

- The nature and quality of the relationship with the person or people involved.
- Their emotional and spiritual state at the time of the offense.
- Your emotional state at the time of the offense.
- The nature of what was said or done.

I can admit these factors do not always prevent me from feeling offended, but they have increased my insight on how to respond. Furthermore, they minimize the lure to respond in ungodly ways.

God, thank You for highlighting this area of my life that needs work. I will extend grace to people before jumping to conclusions. Give me the wisdom to foresee some offenses and the wisdom to know how to respond, even if that means not responding.

Day 29

ORPHANED

To become an orphan (without parents, usually due to death).

God in His holy dwelling is a father of the fatherless
and a champion of widows.
PSALM 68:5

I lost my mother at a time when the rest of my life was flourishing greatly. My mother was a quiet, yet incredibly powerful and beautiful soul. I was blessed to experience the depth of her as a mother, best friend, sister, and sister in Christ. Imagine how my world changed when the only biological parent with whom I ever bonded was gone. There were times when my pain was inconsolable as there seemed to be no words to fully capture the essence of my emotional void. One evening, I went to a remembrance service at a church in a nearby town, and the pastor's wife shared a testimony about losing her parents. As soon as she spoke the word "orphaned," I thought to myself, "that's it!" Tears began to run down my face. That one word fully summarized my sentiments.

Losing a parent is one of the most difficult experiences in human existence. There are so many words, yet there are no words. I've heard it takes years, if not the rest of your lifetime to adjust to the loss. As I have journeyed with so many others in the loss of their parents and now engaging in my own grief process, I began to think of the pain of those who feel orphaned and their parents are still alive. What if you are adopted and don't know your biological parents? Even if you were blessed with loving adoptive parents, many people acknowledge they still have burning questions and desire for their biological parents. What if you never developed a close relationship with your parents? I have experienced and witnessed the effects of this parental dynamic. It's unstable, confusing, lonely, and hurtful because the person who is expected to meet your needs is unwilling and/or unable to do so.

No matter the circumstances that paved the way for your feeling orphaned, there is hope. What are we to do in these cases?

- We acknowledge the deep longing for a connection that only a parent can fill.

- We don't judge ourselves for the ebb and flow of emotions that come expectedly or unexpectedly.

- We make room for God as our father.

God is a father to the fatherless (*and motherless – insertion mine*) (Psalm 68:5). When we accepted Jesus into our lives as Lord and Savior, we were adopted into His family (Eph. 1:5). We are His masterpiece and He wants to preserve (Jer. 49:11) and protect us (Psalm 10:17-18).

God, thank You for being a father to me and knowing my needs before I ask You. I will delight in knowing I am Your child even when my parents forsake me or when my parents are no longer here with me.

Day 30

POWERLESS

Helpless, incapable, ineffective.

*I am able to do all things through Him who
strengthens me.*
PHILIPPIANS 4:13

When circumstances in your life become too overwhelming, do you trust in yourself, or do you doubt yourself? Your answer to this question can shed light on your emotions and behavior. A psychologist named Albert Bandura discovered a concept called self-efficacy, which is your belief that you have the ability to influence outcomes. In other words, how you see yourself has an impact on your motivation and the actions you take (or not take). When you have high self-efficacy, you have confidence that you have some sense of control over outcomes and you are more likely to feel motivated to engage in the behavior necessary to get your desired outcome. In contrast, when you have low self-efficacy, you feel helpless and believe there is nothing you can do (or could have done) to make a difference, and it impacts your mood and behavior. The most crucial part of low self-efficacy is powerlessness and the misconception that other people and factors outside your control have all the power. (e.g., *"I can only be successful if the right people notice me; I failed because the teacher does not like me; I had a bad game because the other team cheated me; They made me mad, so I couldn't control my anger"*).

According to Dr. Bandura, there are several ways we develop self-efficacy like encouragement from significant people in your life, having a history of positive outcomes, seeing other people succeed, and your emotional state. Does this information put your feelings of powerlessness in perspective? Explore when or how your feelings of helplessness began. – Was it through watching other people's failures? Were you put down by people who should have been building you up? Did you have a series of situations with unfavorable outcomes? Are you depressed and lacking confidence in your capacity to make a difference?

All things considered, adding spirituality to the mix complicates things even further. Here's what I mean. Many people wonder why they should even try when God is going to do whatever He wants to do anyway. They see life as happening to them and that God doesn't really listen to prayers. I cannot tell you the number of folks I have counseled who feel powerless when they look around at their circumstances. Heck, I've even had similar thoughts and feelings. Do you feel that way now?

To work through feeling powerless, try reflecting on these truths:

1. God-inspired efforts are not futile: The enemy would have us to draw the conclusion that our efforts are in vain if God does not grant the outcomes we desired and expected. Our faith strengthens by walking in obedience, not by getting certain results. The saying *"Either I win or I learn"* should motivate us to continue on in our God-inspired effort towards our God-given goals.

2. False power is powerless: If we are not careful, our gifts and talents can bring about a false sense of power. Accordingly, God will orchestrate circumstances to remind us that we can only go so far in our own strength. We have to explore whether our feelings of powerlessness indicate we are trying to accomplish goals in our own strength, apart from Him.

3. God is the ultimate authority: It is true that people in certain positions like supervisors, teachers, ministers, police, parents, politicians, doctors, attorneys, and military officers have a degree of power, and some have abused their power. I want to impress upon you that God has not given us a spirit of fear (*of man – addition mine*) and timidity but of power, love, and sound mind (2 Tim. 1:7). Pray for those in leadership, so they do not abuse their role. Additionally, pray for yourself to have a proper perspective of their role, so you don't inappropriately give away the godly power that God has given you.

4. Outcomes are not the only measure of success: When we only focus on outcomes as a measure of our power, it can be discouraging. Outcomes have so many factors that are beyond our control, especially if it involves other people. Try one of the affirmations I prescribe to almost all my patients: *I will give myself credit for my efforts and not just for outcomes.*

God, I feel powerless in my circumstances. Show me if there are any areas of my life where I am trying to move in my own strength in ungodly ways. Help me to be wise in my obedience to You and those in authority. I cast down any thoughts I have about myself that will render me ineffective for the Kingdom. I am thankful that the same power that raised Jesus from the dead is also alive in me.

Day 31

REJECTED

To decline; To shun, exclude, deny approval or acceptance of someone.

The Lord will not reject his people; he will not abandon his special possession.
PSALM 94:14 (NLT)

Like most words, the word "reject(ed)" has several definitions. I summarize them in 2 basic groups: general and relational. In general, rejected means to deny or decline a request or offer.

As I reflect on my life, I am reminded of a time when my application for a certain opportunity was declined. I felt crushed, rejected, and embarrassed. It took a while for me to accept the decision in my heart and once I did, I realized I was not as ready as I initially estimated. The rejection gave me a more accurate picture of myself and the job site. I am thankful to have had the opportunity to refine my skills and eventually, I got a position that was even better. That's not the end of the story, though. The beauty is I am quickly reminded of that feeling when I am around peers who are critical of others in a job setting. This experience keeps me humble and helps me to have patience and compassion towards others, even when I have to decline a request.

Relationally, feeling rejected is the result of someone showing lack of concern or affection toward someone or something. Read about these 3 cases below and see what emotion comes up for you.

1) Hailey is biracial and does not feel accepted by people in either ethnic culture. Hailey wants nothing more than to have a relationship with her mom, but her mom chooses to remain distant.

2) Anthony has always wanted to be accepted and no matter how he tries, he continues to find himself in non-reciprocal relationships.

3) Misty knew for sure she was in a relationship with "The One" until he abruptly ended their relationship and quickly moved on.

My heart just aches for their emotional well-being as I suppose they ended up asking questions like, *"Am I not good enough? Why don't I belong?"*

Can your heart relate to what they are feeling? I'm not sure what or who has rejected you. Maybe you are adopted and have unanswered questions. Maybe your request for a job or loan was denied. Maybe you're seen as the "black sheep of the family," or you have a failed relationship. Maybe you were bullied by the popular crowd, or you were not selected for the fraternity or sorority. Whatever the source of your rejection, I understand how you feel, dear friend. As painful as these experiences were, I am so grateful for them because there were lessons I learned that I would not have otherwise acquired. I hope the following thoughts will both affirm and challenge you.

- The need to be loved and belong are not wrong, so don't pray these feelings away. It's just that our rejection comes when the people who should rightfully care for us don't or when we look for love in the least certain of places.

- Your true validation can only come from God. Examine your heart to see if you're looking for other people to affirm you. Have you given another person or group of people power over your identity and esteem?

- Be reminded of God's unconditional love for you. He loves you for who you are, not for what you do.

God, thank You for loving me, always. Thank You for protecting me from things my natural eyes can't see. Help me find comfort in knowing that You will never abandon me. May I find courage in You even when I feel shunned by others.

Day 32

SAD

Unhappy, gloomy, melancholy.

The Lord is near the brokenhearted; He saves those
crushed in spirit.
PSALM 34:18

How do you typically respond when you're asked how you're feeling? Do you give a generic answer like "*good, okay, fine, blessed,*" even when that is not the case? If so, then maybe you can help me with something. If God is near the brokenhearted, why don't more Christians talk about their sadness? I know I've been there, and I'm a Christian psychologist. How paradoxical is that?

When I revisit the times I've denied my sadness, it was usually around other Christians who would quickly slap me with a Scripture and insinuate that my confessing to sadness was an open door for the enemy to overtake me. These encounters always made me feel worse and question the validity of my feelings. As I began to think deeper about these interactions, I realized some people are uncomfortable with their own emotions, so they tend to minimize or dismiss the sadness of others. I also came to understand that we allow expectations to influence our mood. Thoughts like "*I shouldn't feel sad*" and "*I should be over this by now*" all demonstrate the impact of such expectations.

We have to go deeper to discover the origin of these assumptions and judgments we place on ourselves. Are they the result of your parents, friends, spouse, ministry leaders or other important figures in your life?

Furthermore, I recognized the influence of culture on our moods because it has predetermined what situations warrant sadness and the expiration date for the sadness. Have you noticed that our culture says it's acceptable and understandable to feel sad about death, breakups/divorce, loss of job or home, but only for a moment? The unspoken expectation is that you quickly find the silver lining in the cloud. Anything less than swift triumph indicates whining, ungratefulness, weakness, and lack of faith.

I'm here to remind you it's not a sin to feel sadness nor to communicate it to someone else. Sadness also does not reflect negatively on your faith. Thankfully, I grew to understand there is a difference between expressing my mood and rehearsing or wallowing in it. The keys are found in voicing our feelings to God and to compassionate people. The book of Lamentations in the Bible helps us navigate these moments because one of its themes is sorrow. These kinds of prayers help us to grow emotionally and spiritually as we can cry out to God, ask Him tough questions, and rest in the hope of His mercy. He wants to minister to our crushed spirits.

Through prayer, God can show you who is a safe person to talk to about your problems. Don't subject yourself to a worsening mood by denying your pain. I suppose more people would be drawn to Christianity if we were transparent with our struggles as it would further demonstrate God's power and compassion.

God, I'm feeling sad today because (fill in the blank). I acknowledge my sadness and thank You for being a God I can talk to openly about my feelings. I want to remove the heavy mask of constant happiness. Help me to have peace knowing You will walk me through the discomfort of feeling blue.

Day 33

SUSPICIOUS

Guarded, disbelieving.

Guard your heart above all else, for it is the source of life.
PROVERBS 4:23

A while back, I struck up a conversation with a single parent who told me she enjoyed spending time with her daughter. When I mentioned friendships, she asked, "Why do I need friends when I have siblings?" She went on to say she rarely spent time with extended family. She explained she didn't want to be around them because they would probably talk bad about her after she left. As time passed, I noticed she was very well-liked by others, yet the conversations she made were very polite and impersonal as she kept people at arm's length. She rationalized that although kids at church seemed to love her, it made her uncomfortable because in this day and age, someone could accuse her of being inappropriate with children. What about going to the women's retreat? Well, that wasn't an option because the women will pretend to be her friend and then spread her business. So, I was not surprised when she told me she didn't date because she questioned men's compliments and motives for wanting to get to know her.

Over time, I grew exhausted listening to the mental gymnastics she had to do to protect herself. I longed for her to be more optimistic about interpersonal relationships. Unfortunately, she is not alone in her stance. You're probably feeling that way too if you operate in constant suspiciousness. You're afraid of getting hurt. You're afraid of trying something new. You're afraid to let anyone in. Naturally, many of us feel guarded after being hurt and in some seasons, that approach may even be necessary. However, it's a lot of work to keep that up once the season of threat ends. The challenge in combating these thoughts and feelings is the perceived benefits of being on guard. Yes, you prevent yourself from being hurt but imagine how full your life could be if you allowed genuine people in your circle or if you tried something new. Really, stop and think about that for a minute before you read on.

Now, let's add your faith to the mix of feeling suspicious. How can you thrive as a guarded Christian? It is an oxymoron for us Christians to be suspicious and isolated. Go back and review the 10 Commandments and notice their relational nature (Ex. 20:1-17). God gave us guidelines on our relationship with Him and with others. As a wise steward of your heart, I'm not suggesting that you throw caution to the wind and open yourself up to everyone and anyone. For instance, you wouldn't call a known gossiper for advice in the time of need. What I am encouraging you to realize is that not everyone is out to get you and not everyone has bad intentions. You may not want to or feel ready to take down your wall, and that's fine. Would you at least consider trading your wall for a window? That way, you can let light in, and when it's dark outside, your light can shine too. I can't promise you will never be disappointed again, but the window will at least release you to be able to open it for the right people.

Doesn't God tell us to guard our hearts? Yes, but we don't have to misinterpret what that proverb really means. It doesn't mean for us to shut people out. It means for us to interact with wisdom and use the Word of God as a filter for our actions and relationships. We were not created to be hypervigilant and suspicious 24/7. It's unsustainable and being suspiciousness automatically assumes people's intentions are impure and perceives threats that are not there. If you consider all the roadblocks, detours, and deflections it takes to protect yourself, you eventually end up in a box. That isolated and unloving approach is contrary to God's desire for our lives. The Holy Spirit in us allows our soul to relax because He will help us discern people's motives. We have to look for the good in people, which is found first by acknowledging the good in God and in us.

Oh, one last thing for today. Our relationship with others typically mirrors our relationship with God. Are you guarded with Him, too?

Father, thank You for being trustworthy. Give me the
desire to develop and maintain genuine connections
with You and others. I have been hurt and fear that I
will get hurt again. Heal my heart and remind me that
no matter what happens to me, You will work all things
together for my good. Open the eyes of my heart so I can
recognize and welcome the opportunity to connect with
genuine people and live the abundant life
You have for me.

Day 34

TORMENT

Severe mental pain, anguish, suffering.

Finally brothers, whatever is true, whatever is honorable,
whatever is just, whatever is pure, whatever is lovely,
whatever is commendable – if there is any moral
excellence and if there is any praise – dwell on these things.
PHILIPPIANS 4:8

Imagine being unable to think as clearly, sleep, or concentrate for a period of time. That was me. After a couple of years of freedom, it was back. A tormenting thought and fear that made me physically sick. The thought had been quietly planted many years ago, but it eventually sprouted into a strong fear that I could not seem to shake. It even showed up in my dreams from time to time. I won't go into details about the nature of my torment because it involves people other than me. I don't want to hurt anyone, and those details will distract me and you from the purpose of this devotional entry.

Nevertheless, I'm sure you can relate to my suffering. A majority of people feel tormented by real or perceived mistakes from their past, intrusive images from traumatic experiences, or fears about the future.

What eats away at you? Do you notice how the things that torment you are all based on your thoughts? This truth explains the phrase "battlefield of the mind" popularized by Joyce Meyer, one of the greatest spiritual leaders and teachers of our time. The enemy wants to render us ineffective, so we don't have the mental fortitude and time to walk in our purpose to impact God's Kingdom.

There are different psychological and spiritual explanations for the basis of torment. To fully dissect them is beyond the scope of this book. The main point is that some believe that torment (mental or physical) always points to a sin issue. However, God's word shows us this is not always true. Remember the story about the man who was born blind? The disciples questioned the cause of his blindness and Jesus clarified it was NOT a sin issue (John 9:1-3). This discovery helped me to take a long look at the origin of my own torment, its impact on me, and the weapons I had access to in the Kingdom.

For some, there is actually a biological explanation for the torment they experience. In these cases, it is better to discuss the matter with medical and mental health professionals and spiritual advisors. The bottom line is God is able, period.

In my case, it was solely a spiritual matter. I prayed and sought wise counsel. Instead of continuing to be emotionally paralyzed when the thoughts came up, I began to fight back. I wish I could say that fear has vanished completely, but what I can say is I am torturing those thoughts and feelings right back. Consider applying these strategies to your torment:

- *Check your gates to identify any vulnerabilities.* Are you permitting ungodly thoughts to run wild without addressing them? Are you filling your mind with movies and music that promote darkness?

- *Evaluate your social circle.* Are you encircled by other tormented people or people who help you rehearse your painful past or fearful future?
- *Get in God's word to find out what He says about the issue.*
- *Put on your belt of truth.* Stand firm by dwelling on what is true, noble, honorable, pure, just, lovely, and commendable.

God, my mind and emotions are plagued with torment right now. I'm robbed of the peace You gave me because I have been dwelling on the past or fretting the future. I renounce any ungodly spiritual access and influence on my mind and emotions. Thank You that my soul is relaxed, and I am walking in Your peace.

Day 35

UNAPPRECIATED

Thankless, unrecognized, undervalued.

Work willingly at whatever you do, as though you were
working for the Lord rather than for people.
COLOSSIANS 3:23 (NLT)

There was a popular song in the mid-2000s called "Unappreciated" sang by the group Cherish. The lyrics stated, *"I'm feeling really unappreciated. You takin' my love for granted, babe and I don't know how much more I can take from you."* Although this is a love song, the sentiment of feeling unappreciated is one that most people have felt at some point in their lives. You work so hard, but your efforts go unnoticed. You give so much, and your time is not respected. I'm sure you can agree that being valued feels good. When I get a genuine compliment, I feel pleased, seen, and inspired. Though I don't thrive on external recognition, it's nice to be thanked or valued. What about you? How do you feel when you get compliments? How is your mood impacted when you don't receive them?

When you feel unappreciated, something I recommend is looking at the motivations of your heart. Let me show you what I mean. I knew a man who was truly an excellent worker. He was smart, creative, and productive. The problem was that he would metaphorically pretend his hands were tied behind his back and voluntarily add projects to his already overloaded plate. Then he would go around complaining that others were piling work on him. However, when he was recognized and thanked "for being the only one to volunteer," you could see him gloat in the praise.

At the root of his behavior was a heart's desire to be recognized by others. The desire wasn't wrong; it was his way of engaging in manipulative tactics to get the praise that was troublesome. We must examine the motives of our hearts and take a deeper look into our self-worth. Our key verse shows us the Bible gives us instruction to work unto the Lord. If our sole purpose in doing is to be appreciated by people, we have already received our full reward. In other words, we would rather God recognize and promote us rather than relying on others or promoting ourselves. Furthermore, if your self-worth is contingent upon getting external appreciation, it's an indication that you've got some heart work to do.

Equally important is considering whether you show appreciation to others. Not the I'm-doing-it-to-show-you-how-I-like-it kind of appreciation, but a genuine acknowledgement of who they are and what they mean to you. When I engage in couple and family therapy, one of the assignments I give them is to express gratitude to one another. That seems simple enough, right? Well, you would be surprised to see people look awkwardly at one another, squirm in their seats, and laugh nervously as they give and receive positive comments. We must not get so consumed with having our efforts noticed that we don't take the time to genuinely praise others. We often notice good things about others, but we don't verbalize them because we have been so conditioned to voice complaints.

I know what you're thinking. You have a pure heart and still feel invisible to those around you. It's like people only recognize you when you are doing something for them. In this case, I'd say it's okay to voice your concerns and needs. People may not know your love language, or they may not be communicating appreciation in a way that feeds your soul. My prayer is that those in your environment sincerely recognize you and see the depths of your heart and you can do the same for others.

> *God, I appreciate Your omniscience and omnipresence.*
> *Forgive me for all the times I rush through life without*
> *stopping to appreciate who You are and what You*
> *have done in my life. Show me any ungodly desires for*
> *appreciation in my heart and help me to find ways to*
> *acknowledge others.*

Day 36

UNWORTHY

Undeserving, without value, not good enough.

*And the very hairs on your head are all numbered. So
don't be afraid; you are more valuable to God than a
whole flock of sparrows.*
LUKE 12:7

It saddens my heart when I see people struggle with feeling unworthy of love from themselves, others, or God. As I dig deeper,
I learn that it's based on the belief that something they have done or
was done to them makes them invaluable and undeserving of love.
I ask you the same question I've asked them and myself. *What are
the consequences of feeling unworthy?* Here are some of the common
realizations to this question:

- Tolerating mistreatment from others.
- Lacking boundaries.
- Pushing away people who genuinely love you or want to get
  to know you.
- Decreased ability to fully embrace God's grace and forgive-
  ness.
- Increased negative self-talk.
- Conforming to the demands of an unhealthy environment.

- Not voicing your opinion on matters of importance to you.
- Looking for others to validate you.
- Ruminating on your mistakes.
- Procrastinating or never pursuing goals.

Isn't this list sad? My purpose in having you look at this list is not to make you feel worse. I want you to get a fuller picture of the ways feeling unworthy stunts your relationships and growth. Through your tears, I want you to know you are worthy and you deserve love. I want you to saturate every cell in your body with God's love for you. He loved you enough to send His Son to die for your sins. He was the ultimate sacrifice, so you don't have to be the sacrifice. God thinks You're His masterpiece (Eph. 2:10) and He finds you valuable (Luke 12:6-7).

Listen to or read the lyrics to Anthony Brown's song, "Worth." Meditate on your value today.

God, thank You for loving me and forgiving me. I acknowledge that I am worthy. Help me to begin to walk in Your identity for me.

Day 37

USED

Take advantage of, misuse for one's own advantage.

Bless them that curse you, and pray for them which despitefully use you.
LUKE 6:28

I cannot begin to count how many times I felt used and whined to God about it. I'll explain why. Some of my spiritual gifts are exhortation, wisdom, and discernment, which draws a lot of people to me when they are in distress even outside the context of a professional therapeutic relationship. I feel so fulfilled and useful when I am able to speak life into people and see real change in their mood and life circumstances. It's amazing! The downside is feeling used when those same people were inconsiderate of my needs or when they tossed me aside when they were on the up and up. It bothered me greatly. Does that make sense?

Before I go on, I want to know how have people used you. Is it for your gifts, time, resources, connections, money, body, status, etc.? Whatever it is, I'm sorry you have landed on this page of the book. I'm going to let you in on two eye-openers that I think might be beneficial to you. I promise you; I won't feel used. ☺

One day, I was pondering on yet another person in my life who seemed dismissive and disinterested at a time when I really needed an ear. The Holy Spirit quietly dropped the word *"equipped"* into my spirit and left me to chew on that for a while. As I researched the word,

I saw that it means to perfect or supply. In my study, God revealed to me many of the people I looked to were not equipped to give me what I needed despite my being able to pour into them. That was so freeing as it released me from having unrealistic expectations of others. It does not mean anything negative about them as they may be gifted in different areas than me. It is also possible they are not equipped due to lack of resources, experience, and/or emotional/spiritual maturity. Either way, that epiphany changed the game for me.

Another truth came through a revelation about the principle of reaping and sowing found in Galatians 6:7. We reap *what* we sow, not necessarily *where* we sow. God may choose the same person to bless me, or He may choose to bless me another way. After having this epiphany, I was free to look to God and His sovereignty to repay what I have sown.

So, I ask you these 2 questions: 1) Is the person who used you equipped to give you what you need? 2)What are your motives for giving, doing, serving? Our key verse tells us to pray for those who despitefully use us. This Scripture implies that our intentions are pure so that we can serve others genuinely and pray for them in love. Maybe they have good intentions or maybe they don't. Nevertheless, you are covered since you have acted in love.

God, thank You for never mistreating me. As I heal from feeling used, give me wisdom about how to and with whom I'm spending my time, talent/gifts, resources, emotions, etc. Show me how to draw boundaries where needed. Forgive me for expecting from others what they are not equipped to give.

Day 38

VENGEFUL

Spiteful, vindictive, unforgiving.

Friends, do not avenge yourselves: instead, leave room
for His wrath. For it is written: Vengeance belongs to Me;
I will repay, says the Lord.
ROMANS 12:19

How sweet it is to repay someone who has wronged you! The thought alone can often bring a sense of relief. In our fantasy, we assume we will feel much better after we set the person straight, if we did to them what they've done to us or our loved ones. In psychology, we called this *affective forecasting*, which is foretelling how we will feel in the future after a particular event. Research indicates we are not very good at it. We tend to misconstrue how the situation will play out by overlooking any aspects that are contrary to our imagination. Furthermore, we assume the emotion we predict will be long-lasting. I suppose these findings explain why I did not feel the way I anticipated after I took some matters into my own hands. I assumed I would feel vindicated and for a moment, I did feel that way. Eventually, the feeling faded, and I began to wonder to myself if it was even worth it. The result was carrying the weight of double emotional baggage: the initial hurt and the regret of avenging myself. Conversely, things turned out much better when I waited on God to handle situations. Although, I still felt the sting of the offense, it seemed easier to manage because I had peace with God. I released God to do His work in His timing.

"His timing."

Does that phrase make you cringe? When somebody has wronged us, we grow impatient if God seems slow to keep His word. We feel upset when it seems the other person has gotten away, and he/she is living happily ever after. It won't hurt us to help God out a little, right? Our key verse reminds us that God says "vengeance is mine, I will repay." I believe the Apostle Paul, who authored Romans, knew that our natural response is to retaliate and defend ourselves when someone hurts us. However, he encourages us to live a Christian life contrary to our nature by demonstrating love in action. I don't think our struggle is believing God can't repay. I think it lies in the fact that we aren't sure *when* or *if* He will do it. Before you attempt to settle the score in your own life, take some time to contemplate your answers to the questions below:

- Do you expect that God *immediately* avenges you?
- Do you expect God to pay them back according to your standards and measurement?
- Do you expect the other person will feel the same pain you feel if you take matters into your own hands?

God, I'm hurting and I'm tempted to strike back. Please help me to grasp and treasure the grace You bestow on me by not giving me what I deserve. I want to trust in You and Your timing. Bless me with a forgiving spirit, so I am free to love and live according to Your word.

Day 39

VULNERABLE

Weak, exposed, susceptible to being emotionally or physically wounded exposed.

For when I am weak, then I am strong.
2 CORINTHIANS 12:10

Patient: "*Doc, you're not getting in my head.*"

Me: "*That's okay. I'd rather see what's in your heart anyway.*"

Patient: "*I don't care what you say. You're not getting in my head.*"

This was the initial theme of the therapy work I did with one of my patients. I didn't take his comments to heart as I understood they were coming from a place of pain, and what he really wanted to ask is, "*Can I trust you?*" I knew he was trying to protect himself from feeling emotionally vulnerable and I was ready for the long haul.

I get it. Vulnerability is uncomfortable. Who wants to feel exposed and fragile? Our gut reaction is to protect the ego by attacking or rejecting others or by denying and avoiding our true feelings. Some people define vulnerability as a demonstration of weakness. I see it as just the opposite due to the fact that expressing vulnerability takes an incredible amount of courage. Vulnerability is about being known and seen in the moment. It means to come out of emotional hiding. How do you hide your emotions? Is it through avoidance?

Sarcasm? Providing canned answers to intimate questions? Deflecting? Criticizing others? Staying busy?

Before you close the book due to discomfort, allow me to normalize your sentiments. Everyone has vulnerabilities. The power lies in how we express (or not express) them. It can be the difference between a cordial and a close relationship. Like most people, you may fear abandonment or rejection or being seen as weak. You probably worry about getting hurt after being exposed emotionally. I can't deny there is a risk in being vulnerable, but there is also truth, peace, and opportunity for connection with yourself, God, and others. In fact, we can't have true intimacy without it.

To begin to work towards increased vulnerability, I propose a few steps:

- Ask yourself, *"What do I fear about being vulnerable?"*
- Begin practicing vulnerability by talking openly with God about your fears and concerns.
- Pray for discernment about safe people to trust with your frailties.

I'm sure you want to know what happened with the patient I mentioned earlier. Well initially, he opened up to me with what I call "test problems." These are the surface-level concerns some people talk about first but aren't the real issues. The goal is to see if it's safe to be vulnerable with deeper troubles. Once he began to trust that I would respond with empathy, he eventually disclosed his hurt, shame, and fears. It was wonderful to see his confidence rise as he took appropriate risks in sharing his true thoughts and feelings with me and then with others. I was happy to watch him come to understand that just because you *feel* weak does not mean you *are* weak. It's a risky, yet beautiful process. Trust me.

I want to leave you with these thoughts. Jesus was the best model of vulnerability when He paid the ultimate price for us. He wants you to know that articulating your needs does not make you a needy person. God put needs in us, so He can fill those desires Himself or through others (Phil. 4:19).

Remember this: When you feel weak, that is when we are strong in Christ.

God, thank You for sending Jesus to submit to the ultimate vulnerability. Give me the boldness to benefit from more vulnerability in my relationships with You and others.

Day 40

WEARY

Tired, exhausted, especially from waiting.

And let us not be weary in well doing: for in due season
we shall reap, if we faint not.
GALATIANS 6:9 (KJV)

"I'm sick and tired of being sick and tired!"* How many times have you heard or said that? When I reminisce about the moments I was in that place; it was when I was spiritually exhausted from waiting to see the harvest of what I had sown. The journey is already a challenge, but when you look around and perceive the wicked as prosperous, it does something to your spiritual oomph.

My own weary land experiences give me compassion as I've counseled others who feel weary. They ask questions like: *Why has my healing not come yet and I exercise and eat right? Why do I choose to be celibate, but he fornicates and gets the wife? Why should I keep forgiving my spouse when they continue to hurt me? Why do I keep paying my tithes and still there has been no financial breakthrough?"* These are very reasonable questions, and the wearier you feel, the more pointed your questions become over time. You may start to wonder where is God. Does He even see you? Has He forgotten about you?

We all experience moments or season of weariness, and it's physically and emotionally exhausting. It is in these periods when we come to a major fork in the road. Do I go left, right, or keep straight? Before making a decision, look to the following ideas for direction:

1. *Identify the source of your weariness.*

2. *Determine if you are waiting on others to change or to be what only God can be to you.*

3. *Figure out if God has already given you instruction.*

4. *Spend time in rest, fasting, and prayer.*

Please don't empower your weariness to cause you to doubt, abandon the race, or compromise on God's instructions. Just because you want to give up does not mean you have to give up. God is not slack concerning His promise (2 Peter 3:9 KJV). Look up the word "slack," and you'll see it means to move slowly or to lack activity. What this suggests to me the element of time impacts our feelings of weariness. We expect that God should have answered us by now. Our situation should have changed by now. Our key verse tells us to keep going, for there is surely a due season of harvest, change, and relief. Keep pressing through and don't stop short of your victory.

> *God, my soul is weary from this journey. I love You and want to continue in my efforts to do well. Give me strength to wait on You alone and remember that You are a promise-keeper. Your name is great, and thank You for exalting Your word above Your name (Psalm 138:2).*

NOTES:

ANGRY

1. Angry. (n.d). In *Merriam-Webster's online dictionary* (11th ed.). Retrieved from https://www.merriam-webster.com/dictionary/angry and from https://www.merriam-webster.com/dictionary/anger

2. Eleanor Roosevelt quote…Roosevelt, E. (n.d.) *Footprints in your heart*. Retrieved from https://jamiededes.com/2017/02/18/footprints-in-your-heart-a-poem-by-eleanor-roosevelt/

ANXIOUS

Anxious. (2019). In Oxford University Press (OUP). Retrieved from https://www.lexico.com/en/definition/anxious

BETRAYED

Betrayed. (n.d.). Dictionary.com Unabridged. Retrieved from https://www.dictionary.com/browse/betray?s=t

BORED

Bored. (2019). In Oxford University Press (OUP). Retrieved from https://www.lexico.com/en/definition/bored

BURDENED

Burdened. (2019). In Oxford University Press (OUP). Retrieved from https://www.lexico.com/synonym/burden

CONFUSED

1. Confused. (2019). In Oxford University Press (OUP). Retrieved from https://www.lexico.com/synonym/confused
2. Affective Forecasting...Wilson, T. D., & Gilbert, D. T. (2003). Affective forecasting. In M. Zanna (Ed.), *Advances in experimental social psychology,* Vol. 35 (pp. 345-411). New York: Elsevier.
3. Find out more at www.affectiveforecasting.com

CRITICAL

Critical. (2019). In Oxford University Press (OUP). Retrieved from https://www.lexico.com/definition/critical

DESPERATE

Desperate. (n.d). In *Merriam-Webster's online dictionary* (11th ed.). Retrieved from https://www.merriam-webster.com/dictionary/desperate

DEVASTATED

Devastate. (2019). In Oxford University Press (OUP). Retrieved from https://www.lexico.com/definition/devastate

DISTRACTED

1. Distracted. (2019). In Oxford University Press (OUP). Retrieved from https://www.lexico.com/en/definition/distracted

2. For more on depression and PTSD see the National Alliance on Mental Illness (www.nami.org)

DOUBTFUL

Doubtful. (2013). In Roget's 21st Century Online Thesaurus (3rd ed.). Retrieved from https://www.thesaurus.com/browse/doubtful?s=t

EMPTY

Empty. (n.d). In *Merriam-Webster's online dictionary* (11th ed.). Retrieved from https://www.merriam-webster.com/dictionary/empty

ENVIOUS

1. Envious. (2019). In Oxford University Press (OUP). Retrieved from https://www.lexico.com/synonym/envious

2. Study on envy....Nicole E. Henniger & Christine R. Harris (2015) Envy Across Adulthood: The What and the Who, Basic and Applied Social Psychology, 37:6, 303-318, DOI: 10.1080/01973533.2015.1088440

FORGOTTEN

Forgotten. (2019). In Oxford University Press (OUP). Retrieved from https://www.lexico.com/definition/forgotten

GRIEVED

1. Grieve. (2019). In Oxford University Press (OUP). Retrieved from https://www.lexico.com/definition/grieve

2. Kubler-Ross Stages of Grief....Kubler-Ross, E. (1969). On death and dying. New York, NY: Macmillan

3. For more on grief see www.grief.com

GUILTY

1. Guilty. (2019). In Oxford University Press (OUP). Retrieved from https://www.lexico.com/definition/guilty

2. For more on guilt and shame see www.healingshame.com

HATEFUL

Hate. (n.d). In *Merriam-Webster's online dictionary* (11th ed.). Retrieved from https://www.merriam-webster.com/thesaurus/hate

HOPELESS

Hopeless. (n.d). In *Merriam-Webster's online dictionary* (11th ed.). Retrieved from https://www.merriam-webster.com/dictionary/hopeless

IGNORED

Ignored. (2019). In Oxford University Press (OUP). Retrieved from https://www.lexico.com/en/definition/ignored

IMPATIENT

1. Impatient. (2013). In Roget's 21st Century Online Thesaurus (3rd ed.). Retrieved from https://www.thesaurus.com/browse/impatient?s=t

2. "Happiness is getting what we want" quote...Dillow, L. (2007). Calm my anxious heart: A woman's guide to finding contentment. Colorado Springs, CO: Navpress

INCOMPETENT

Incompetent. (n.d). In *Merriam-Webster's online dictionary* (11th ed.). Retrieved from https://www.merriam-webster.com/thesaurus/incompetent

INSECURE

Insecure. (2019). In Oxford University Press (OUP). Retrieved from https://www.lexico.com/en/definition/insecure

IRRITABLE

Irritable. (2019). In Oxford University Press (OUP). Retrieved from https://www.lexico.com/en/definition/irritable

LONELY

Lonely. (n.d). In *Merriam-Webster's online dictionary* (11th ed.). Retrieved from https://www.merriam-webster.com/thesaurus/lonely

LOST

Lost. (2019). In Oxford University Press (OUP). Retrieved from https://www.lexico.com/en/definition/lost

MISUNDERSTOOD

Misunderstood. (2019). In Oxford University Press (OUP). Retrieved from https://www.lexico.com/synonym/misunderstood

NUMB

Numb. (2019). In Oxford University Press (OUP). Retrieved from https://www.lexico.com/synonym/numb

OFFENDED

1. Offended. (n.d). In *Merriam-Webster's online dictionary* (11th ed.). Retrieved from https://www.merriam-webster.com/thesaurus/offended

2. Fundamental Attribution Error...Ross, L. (1977). The intuitive psychologist and his shortcomings: Distortions in the attribution process. In *Advances in experimental social psychology* (Vol. 10, pp. 173-220). New York: Academic Press.

3. For more on fundamental attribution error see...https://www.simplypsychology.org/fundamental-attribution.html

ORPHANED

Orphaned. (n.d). In *Merriam-Webster's online dictionary* (11th ed.). Retrieved from https://www.merriam-webster.com/dictionary/orphaned

POWERLESS

1. Powerless. (2019). In Oxford University Press (OUP). Retrieved from https://www.lexico.com/synonym/powerless

2. Self-efficacy…Bandura, A. (1994). Self-efficacy. In V. S. Ramachaudran (Ed.), Encyclopedia of human behavior (Vol. 4, pp. 71-81). New York: Academic Press. (Reprinted in H. Friedman [Ed.], Encyclopedia of mental health. San Diego: Academic Press, 1998).

3. For more on self-efficacy see https://positivepsychology.com/bandura-self-efficacy/

REJECTED

Rejected. (2019). In Oxford University Press (OUP). Retrieved from https://www.lexico.com/synonym/rejected

SAD

Sad. (2019). In Oxford University Press (OUP). Retrieved from https://www.lexico.com/synonym/sad

SUSPICIOUS

Suspicious. (n.d). In *Merriam-Webster's online dictionary* (11th ed.). Retrieved from https://www.merriam-webster.com/thesaurus/suspicious

TORMENT

Torment. (n.d). In *Merriam-Webster's online dictionary* (11th ed.). Retrieved from https://www.merriam-webster.com/thesaurus/torment

UNAPPRECIATED

1. Unappreciated. (n.d). In *Merriam-Webster's online dictionary* (11th ed.). Retrieved from https://www.merriam-webster.com/thesaurus/unappreciateded

2. Cherish's Unappreciated lyrics…King, N., Williams, C., King, Farrah, King, Fallon, King, Felisha, & Alexander, P. (2006). Unappreciated. On Unappreciated album. Sho'nuff Records and Capital Records.

UNWORTHY

1. Unworthy. (2019). In Oxford University Press (OUP). Retrieved from https://www.lexico.com/synonym/unworthy

2. Worth by Anthony Brown: Brown, A. (2015). Worth. On Everyday Jesus album. Tyscot Records.

USED

Used. (2019). In Oxford University Press (OUP). Retrieved from https://www.lexico.com/en/definition/use

VENGEFUL

1. Vengeful. (n.d). In *Merriam-Webster's online dictionary* (11th ed.). Retrieved from https://www.merriam-webster.com/thesaurus/vengeful

2. Affective Forecasting…Wilson, T. D., & Gilbert, D. T. (2003). Affective forecasting. In M. Zanna (Ed.), *Advances*

in experimental social psychology, Vol. 35 (pp. 345-411). New York: Elsevier.

3. Find out more at www.affectiveforecasting.com

VULNERABLE

Vulnerable. (n.d). In *Merriam-Webster's online dictionary* (11th ed.). Retrieved from https://www.merriam-webster.com/dictionary/vulnerable and from https://www.merriam-webster.com/thesaurus/vulnerable

WEARY

Weary. (n.d). In *Merriam-Webster's online dictionary* (11th ed.). Retrieved from https://www.merriam-webster.com/thesaurus/weary

ACKNOWLEDGEMENTS

I would like to thank God for my life and for the experiences that laid the foundation for this book. I also thank God for the gift of Jesus' humanity and for leaving us with His Word to help us navigate the tough moments in life. Writing this book was both challenging and rewarding because I was living and reliving the emotions as I wrote it. I am delighted in the completion of this book and cannot wait to hear the awesome testimonies of those who read it.

I am especially grateful for my brother, Quaylon, and extended family and friends who have loved, encouraged, and supported me along the way. I'm so blessed to have each of you in my life and your enthusiasm about the book kept me inspired.

Ms. Patricia Gary, I could not have been blessed with a better godmother. You are truly one of a kind.

Special thanks to Mrs. Nicole C. Calhoun, a gem in my life. Words can scarcely express my appreciation of you. Thank you for being a friend, accountability partner, and awesome woman of God. Your excitement about this project was motivational.

Another sincere thanks to Dr. Felicia Fisher. I'm grateful for the professional relationship that has flourished into a friendship. I appreciate your feedback on various aspects of my work.

Mr. Inioluwa Gabriel, your comments and critique of my book were priceless and gave me the final confirmation I needed. Many blessings to you, sir!

To the women in my life group: Thank you for being real and relatable women of God. I'm so glad we met and I am grateful for your support and opinions.

I would also like to acknowledge my patients, who trust me with the privilege of walking with them as they journey towards emotional wholeness. I cherish the time we have spent and value the lessons I have learned from you.

Finally, I want to thank my son, Quincyn who is wise well-beyond his years. Thank you for letting me pick your brain. You are my treasure and a true manifestation of Psalm 127:3. In God, the world is yours, my dear.

ABOUT THE AUTHOR

Photo Credit: Lens_zee

Dr. QuaVaundra Perry is a board-certified and Christian psychologist, speaker, and consultant who is passionate about applying Biblical truths to free people from emotional bondage. She is founder and owner of a private practice dedicated to serving people who want to be excellent without being perfect. Dr. Perry's expertise has been seen in national media outlets such as *The Oprah Magazine, Elite Daily, Cosmopolitan,* and *Therapy for Black Girls Podcast.*

Dr. Perry lives in Dallas, Texas with her family and favorite shih tzu, Marble. She is an active member in her church and community.

Connect with Dr. Perry at www.drqperry.com and on Instagram @drqperry.

Made in the USA
Coppell, TX
09 January 2021

47810955R00075